Praise for Kasper Hauser's *SkyMaul*

"... a hilarious and wildly inventive spoof ..."
— *Time Out New York*

"Wicked funny ..."
— *San Francisco Chronicle*

"... it might be the funniest thing you read this year ..."
— *Marketplace* (Public Radio International)

"... a note-perfect, naughty takeoff ..."
— *Penthouse*

"... wet-your-pants funny ..."
— *boingboing.net*

"The perfect send-up ..."
— *Salon.com*

"... bang-up hilarious ... Move over, *National Lampoon*."
— *The Seattle Times*

"... brilliantly funny ..."
— *Pittsburgh Post-Gazette*

"Kasper Hauser get kudos for taking [*SkyMall*] to new levels of absurdity."
— *The Village Voice*

"... madly funny, full of wild invention ..."
— George Saunders

Weddings of the Times

A Parody

The Kasper Hauser Comedy Group

Rob Baedeker
Dan Klein
James Reichmuth
John Reichmuth

THOMAS DUNNE BOOKS
ST. MARTIN'S GRIFFIN
NEW YORK

THOMAS DUNNE BOOKS
An imprint of St. Martin's Press.

WEDDINGS OF THE TIMES. Copyright © 2009 by The Kasper Hauser
Comedy Group. All rights reserved. Printed in the United States of
America. For information, address St. Martin's Press, 175 Fifth Avenue,
New York, N.Y. 10010.

www.thomasdunnebooks.com
www.stmartins.com

Library of Congress Cataloging-in-Publication Data

Weddings of the Times : a parody / Kasper
Hauser Comedy Group.—1st ed.
        p. cm.
    ISBN-13: 978-0-312-38091-5 (alk. paper)
    ISBN-10: 0-312-38091-7 (alk. paper)
    1. Weddings—Humor. 2. Newspapers—Sections, columns, etc.—
Weddings. 3. New York times--Parodies, imitations, etc. 4. American
wit and humor. I. Kasper Hauser Comedy Group.
PN6231.W37W43 2009
818'.60708093543--dc22

                                                    2009006933

First Edition: June 2009

10 9 8 7 6 5 4 3 2 1

designed by:
Vince Bohner

contributing designer:
Brad Rhodes

head photographer:
Julie Caskey

original artwork:
James Yamasaki

Foreword

by John Hodgman

When the newspapers are finally defeated by the computers, we will not only lose an important source of very flammable material that stains our fingers, but also three unique human emotions:

First, the reassuring calm of the Funny Pages ("It comforts me to know that Dagwood Bumstead is immortal, and no one looks at him funny just because he wears clothes from the thirties and has deformed hair. I wonder if he is a Highlander?").

Second, the sheer awful panic of the Obituaries ("But wait! No one is really immortal. All of these people died. This is terrible! This is as bad as reading For Better or For Worse, the Canadian comic strip in which everyone ages in real time, and then their dog died.").

And finally, the happy two minutes of hate we call The Wedding Pages ("Go on and grin, you damn preppies. You're not immune! You will die, too. Just like a Canadian dog.").

I cannot tell you how many Sundays I passed enjoying these comforting rituals before I stopped reading newspapers for good (they were getting into my head). And always, it was the third I enjoyed the most.

I was poor then, having moved to New York with nothing but a degree in literary theory and firm convictions that life owed me a living. I ended up with a job tearing out pages from one book and taping them into another all day, and then retiring to my girlfriend's apartment, which was very small. It was basically a sink and a bad fridge with some floorboards around them holding up some cast-off furniture and a Cézanne print.

We tried to make a life there: she, I, her roommate, the guy who was crashing on the sofa with no legs, and the various friends we would invite over for our sad, ridiculously ambitious nine-course weekend dinners in which we would cook a gigantic turkey and attempt to carve it with the only unused butter knife.

It was around that time of fright and yearning that my girlfriend first introduced me to The Wedding Pages. Perhaps she was trying to drop a hint, but I took it differently. Here were people actually beginning adult lives, instead of woefully faking it, as we were. They had planned well, majored in finance, or better, were at that very moment in the process of fulfilling the American dream: marrying into money.

Their parents, who sat on boards and foundations and/or oversaw arts centers in East Hampton, did not worry about them. They did not worry about anything.

I was jealous at first. And then I felt something else. There is a German word, I trust, for the feeling they inspired in me, but I do not know what it is. Not *schadenfreude*. Not pleasure taken in another's unhappiness, but rather the relief I felt considering the unhappiness I imagined for these smiling couples. That as time wore on, they would age as well, and suffer. This brief moment of newspaper glamour would fade, replaced by countless other photos full of the same hope and self-congratulation and soft, cable knit sweaters. And this was hilarious to me, as I was young and cruel.

Now I am older, and no longer quite as defensive and fearful (I am on television). Newspapers are disappearing. And also, I am married, and we never did get our picture in the paper for it. And I regret it.

For I look at The Wedding Pages differently now. Yes, they are as pompous as they are banal, and Kasper Hauser understands these are but two keys to the Gordian knot of comedy. But what the authors of this book know well, and which I am only now beginning to understand, is how brave these people are.

In this collection, Kasper Hauser reminds us that a wedding announcement is a window into the most goofball daydream a couple can have about itself. To write out your own romance novel, even in clipped newspaper prose, and give it to the world to see is incredibly, ridiculously courageous. It might as well be accompanied by every picture of a horse the bride had ever drawn in grade school, and every D&D character the groom had ever rolled. It is as foolhardy and beautiful as, well, actually getting married.

Obviously the weddings in these books are made up. But even at their most absurd, Kasper Hauser is never cruel. These are not parodies, but little human stories, full of want and hope, even when they involve falconry. And so even though these are not real couples, I am rooting for them, the way I root for all married couples now, and I do not want them to die. And thanks to Kasper Hauser, they will not. They will be immortal, Dagwood-style, caught in that frozen moment of hope forever, smiling like morons, happy.

That is all.

Weddings of the Times

from

WEDDINGS of THE TIMES
BY
KASPER HAUSER

Catherine Doyle, Alfred Park

Catherine Doyle married Alfred Park on Sunday evening at the Woodfield Country Club in Boca Raton.

The bride, 26, graduated *magna cum laude* from Georgetown. The groom, 34, graduated *summa cum laude* from Brown. The bride's father, Eugene Doyle, graduated *egregia cum laude* from the University of Washington and his mother, Kate Doyle, graduated *double platinum cum laude* from Wayne State.

Her grandfather graduated *the harder they cum laude* from Texas A&M. Her uncle graduated *cumma cumma cumma cumma cumma chameleon laude* from the University of Colorado.

The bride's brother, Lewis Doyle, graduated *pre-cum laude* from the University of Stockholm.

The groom's father, Bruce, graduated *cumfortably numb laude* from Cal State Fullerton. The best man graduated *cumpire strikes back laude* from the College of Outer Space. The best man's grandfather graduated *viagra cum laude* from Hofstra.

Amanda Parker, Terry Marks

Amanda Parker and Terry Marks were married Sunday at the Three Rivers Shopping Center in Pittsburgh, Pa. Thomas Vowell performed the ceremony.

Ms. Parker, 24, is a former patent secretary for the law firm of Derrick & Coughlon. She is now a zombie, an undead person who got that way from being bitten by another zombie.

She is the daughter of Lucia and Sanford Parker of Latrobe, Pa. Her father is a lawyer in Latrobe specializing in land use and mineral rights. Her mother is retired as the editor of *Country Farm House* magazine.

The groom, 33, is a former art professor at New York University. He is also a zombie.

He is the son of Barbara and Abraham Marks of Palm Springs, Ca. His father is retired as a biochemist with ClorGen; his mother is a volunteer docent at the Pane Museum of Fine Art in Palm Desert, Ca.

Neither the bride nor the groom can be killed unless their head is destroyed.

Caroline Hanson, Dean Van Wyck

Caroline Hanson was married to Dean Van Wyck on Saturday at the Peach Tree farm in Scarsdale, NY.

The bride, 33, wore a strapless white Vera Wang wedding gown.

The bridegroom, 38, wore tight-fitting purple breeches, a white silk shirt, a fox-fur mantle, and a livery collar from which was suspended a diamond the size of a walnut. His wide-sleeved doublet gave emphasis to his upper body, which was accentuated with shoulder pads. Mr. Van Wyck's padded codpiece was stuffed with jewels and weapons; he carried a staff made of silver and bedecked with topaz.

"There was obviously some of kind of miscommunication," said the bride.

Caroline Allerton, Gregory Winslow

Caroline Allerton and Gregory Winslow were married on Sunday at Calgary Church in Manhattan. The Reverend Scott Tilley performed the ceremony.

Mr. Winslow, 28, met Ms. Allerton, 26, while attending Harvard University, where both graduated *summa cum laude*.

Ms. Allerton is a Daughter of the American Revolution, as is Mr. Winslow's mother. The bride's father is a Son of the American Revolution.

The American Revolution is also the groom's uncle.

"The American Revolution used to come 'round," said the bride's mother, "He had the stereo, he had the flashy clothes, he had the nice van. A lot of ladies used to party with the American Revolution, OK?"

Brittany Dowling,
Glen Dorio

Glen Dorio, a scuba diving instructor, and Brittany Dowling, a professional photographer, held an underwater wedding ceremony in a shark cage near the Dyer islands off the coast of South Africa.

The bride and groom are survived by their parents, Joan and Arlen Dorio, and Briana and Delray Dowling.

Penelope and Odysseus

STATE OF THE UNION

20 Years Later

When Odysseus, King of Ithaca, was first married to his bride Penelope (see "Vows," 759 B.C.), he built her a special bed. "One of the legs of it was made out of an olive tree," he said. "I don't know. I just thought it was different."

But the couple's marital bliss was short-lived. The warrior went off to battle, for 10 years, and then spent another 10 years trying to get back home.

"Many shitty things happened," he said, sipping some mead on his sun deck. "I don't want to get started. Cyclops? Yes. Happened. Lotus eaters? 100% true. My guys ate the Cattle of Helios. Then I had some health problems. Lost my house, went to Hades, got into Tai Chi, got involved with a nympho, got clean, did some time …"

Odysseus's wife wondered if she'd ever see the Trojan War hero again.

And then there were the suitors.

"There were many," she affirmed. "I pretended to weave a burial sleeping bag for O.'s dad, Laertes, and I told the suitors I'd choose one of them when I finished."

"But every night she'd unweave the sleeping bag," chimed in the old campaigner.

"We killed a lot of people."

Eventually Odysseus did return home, disguising himself as a junkie and slaying the suitors with a bow and arrow, with help from his son, Telemachus.

"We killed a lot of people," he laughed.

But Penelope was not so sure it was really her husband who'd come back. "I tested him by asking my servant to move the bed," she remembered.

"But I told her he couldn't," Odysseus added. "Because I built that bed. It was a tree bed! Ha ha! I'm a genius. Born and bred. No one but a genius would have known how to make that bed and fake people out and all the other stuff I did on my journey."

Penelope added, "I did have moments of crisis while he was gone. At one point I asked Artemis to kill me—But then I also maybe wanted to marry one of the suitors?"

"Which one?" asked Odysseus.

"Demoptolemus," blushed Penelope. "The singer-song-writer."

"Yeah, he was a nice-looking kid," reminisced the bride-groom. "I kind of wish I hadn't slain him."

The battle-weary hero paused and looked at his wife. "Slayed?" he said. "Is it slayed or slain?"

Regina Harrison, Jimmy Holgren

Regina Harrison and Jimmy Holgren were married Sunday at the Zen Buddhist Peace Center in Carmel, Calif. The ceremony was performed by Buddhist Monk Budiman Prang.

The bride, 26, is studying to be a massage therapist.

The bridegroom, 27, is a yoga instructor and peace activist.

The day of the wedding was selected by an astrologer based on its auspiciousness. Before the ceremony, the assembled monks chanted. The guests then said the Vandana, Tisarana, and Pancasila readings, after which the couple lit incense sticks and candles around a Buddha statue. Vows and rings were exchanged using the Sigilovdda Sutta as a guide.

Immediately following the ceremony, the D.J. played "A Whole New World" from the *Aladdin* soundtrack and pretty much blasted everyone back to fucking reality again.

Emily Harcutt,
Michael Cosley

Emily Harcutt and Michael Cosley are to be married on Friday at Chesapeake Grove, S.C. Father Walter Bramley will officiate.

The couple, both bumper sticker writers, met in San Diego, Ca. at BumperCon 2005, the largest annual gathering of bumper sticker fans, authors, and collectors. Ms. Harcutt, 28, first noticed Mr. Cosley, 43, at the keynote address given by industry visionary Ronald Wilcox, renowned scribe of the bumper stickers "I'm not as think as you stoned I am" and "God is coming and BOY is she pissed."

Ms. Harcutt and Mr. Cosley later formed a business together, scoring big hits with such stickers as "Yes, this is my truck, and no I won't help you move!" and "Free Mumia!* (*with purchase of cheeseburger and large drink)." Their firm, BumperSchnitzel, also won BSIA Awards for their stickers "My other child is an honor student" and "Keep honking: I'm loaded and I have a blowgun."

Julie Cashman,
Hiroji Kamata

Deep cultural differences have not kept Hiroji Kamata and Julie Cashman apart. The two will be married on Sunday at the Asian Art Museum in Los Angeles.

Ms. Cashman, 28, is from Connecticut and can trace her roots to the Pilgrims on the Mayflower.

Mr. Kamata, 31, traces his family origins to a small island north of Okinawa that practices a different form of *Bushido*, the traditional code that guides the life of a warrior.

"On our island," says Mr. Kamata, "a father does not pass on to his son the family *Katana*, or 'Samurai sword'; instead he bestows on the son a *Buresuto Ke-ki*, a 'breast pastry' or what Americans would call a titty-cake."

"Watching Hiroji's titty-cake ceremony was one of the most moving moments of my life," said the bride. "I'm one of the first Westerners to have ever witnessed it."

"I got a good one," says Mr. Kamata, "Vanilla buttercream. Huge nipples."

Gina Flushing, Kyle Pearson

Gina Flushing and Kyle Pearson were married Saturday at the Holdale State Park in Carson City, Nev.

The couple were arrested during the ceremony by the officiant, Lt. Sheldon Graeber of the Carson City Police Department.

The bridegroom is wanted for money laundering; the bride has been a fugitive for six years, evading charges of arson and skink-poaching on federal preserves.

"This is the CCPD's Wedding Sting Division," said Lt. Graeber. "We track these couples who are at-large and we lure them in with amazing wedding deals—limos, Nona Ha gowns, chocolate ganache cakes, gazebos, fancy soaps, puppy baskets; that kind of thing—and then, during the vows, we cuff 'em and stuff 'em."

WEDDING MEDICAL EMERGENCIES

Weddings are meant to be one of life's most special gatherings. But with a mixture of young and old guests, plentiful food and drink, and more and more exotic venues, weddings can become danger zones. That's why modern brides and grooms need to be ready with quick fixes for wedding medical emergencies.

 DROWNING Pull your father-in-law out of the pool and hose him down. Remove his wetsuit and put him in a sleeping bag. Using a blower, perform some CPR.

 CHOKING Sweep the cake off the tonsils in an arcing "U" motion and whip it to the side. Listen to the nose. If there is still no breathing, flip the man into a wheelbarrow position and perform nine percussive bear hugs.

 BEE STING ALLERGY Pour soda water on the bee to neutralize it, and then flick it into a wall. Give the allergic person his shot, being careful not to give yourself any of the shot. If there is leftover shot, spray it out, or give the rest of it to the allergic person.

 FALL If a person has fallen, there is no cure, but you can do things to make the person more comfortable while waiting for the outcome. Feed the person the same as what any other guests get: treat them as equals.

 BROKEN LEG Reduce the fracture if it is displaced. Use gaffer's tape and a golf bag as a splint while you wait for the white van.

HEART ATTACK
Remember, "O" stands for Offer the person something to eat or drink: the same as what other guests are getting. "P" is for CPR if needed.

SHARK ATTACK
Scoop the top half of the person into the catamaran and hose them down. Put them into a sleeping bag and pressurize.

DIABETIC COMA
When the person wakes up, many years may have passed. Try to dress like you did back when the coma started and shave your beard if it's long. Don't tell them the year right off the bat, but later, when they're ready.

SPROLLEN ANKLE
A cold fudge ball on the medial malleolus should help the swelling. DO NOT try to spin the foot all the way around.

POISONING
The classic remedy for poisoning is to give the exact opposite of what the person took: the antidote. For example, if they ate pesticides, you would give them the opposite of that.

NAUSEA AND VOMITING
First, look for causes: is the person pregnant? Is everyone who ate the same thing pregnant? Find clues then work your way back.

GUNSHOT OR STAB WOUNDS
First, shoot the person who shot or stabbed your guest. Then treat the wound like you would any other.

BLUNT TRAUMA
Did a person throw a full beer can at another person's back? A cold compress should do. If a person has many bruises, they should sit the wedding out.

Tracy Schechner, Tom Jameson,

Love sprang from the most terrifying and trying of experiences for Tom and Tracy Jameson, who were married on Saturday at Shepherd's Flock Baptist Church in Houston.

"When you're not sure if you're going to live or die," said the bridegroom, 31, "all you can do is just hang in there and pray."

And pray they did, while at sea on a small raft for 51 days with three others after their cruise ship capsized in the Indian Ocean.

"We got to know each other real fast," said Mr. Jameson. "We saw sides of each other that would only come out under such strain."

"I ate Tom's old roommate," said the bride, 29.

"Yeah, but that's what I mean," said the bridegroom. "No way she would have done that if we hadn't been out there basically starving. But she still blames herself."

"I ate two other people, too," said Tracy, "I have a people-eating disorder."

Heather Wilson, Darren Steegan

Heather Wilson, daughter of Mr. and Mrs. Mark Wilson, of New Haven, was married yesterday to Darren Steegen, son of Mr. and Mrs. Toby Steegen of Wahasset, N.Y.

The bride, 28, is the former national women's tennis champion and currently works as a Broadway actress and fashion model for Armani. She deferred enrollment at Yale University in order to serve as a Dallas Cowboys cheerleader from 1997 to 2001.

The bridegroom, 38, resides with his parents in Wahasset. He is a part-time student at Icaba Community College, where he studies the Internet. The elaborate ceremony took place in Mr. Steegen's mind.

The couple met on a remote tropical island where Ms. Wilson was sunbathing. She was at first startled by Mr. Steegen, but then gave herself to him freely. All of this was in his mind.

Marta Green,
Nate Sirota

Marta Green and Nate Sirota were married on Friday at the Sun Horizons Convention Center in Sarasota, Florida. Rabbi Tom Goldwitz officiated.

The couple met in the online virtual world known as Second Life. Mr. Sirota's screen character, or "avatar," is a four-legged centaur with a rippling human torso and the arms and head of "James Bond" actor Daniel Craig.

"The instant I saw him, I fell in love," said the bride. "I'm a huge D&D girl, plus I love Daniel Craig."

"You should see her avatar," said the groom. "It's a dolphin with a human tongue. Plus she's got wings and she's a surgeon."

Asked how they planned to spend their honeymoon, the couple replied, "Cyberlingus and pixellatio."

Marcy Florman, Kurt Kerr

Marcy Florman and Kurt Kerr were married Saturday at the Civic Center in Burlington, Vt. The ceremony was performed by their longtime friend James Stamsted.

Ms. Florman, 31, is a cashier at Vicky's You Check 'Em in Burlington.

Mr. Kerr, 39, is the assistant manager of a consignment store called AAAAA Pawn in Burlington.

Editors' note: This couple was included in the announcements because we see a lot of potential here. There is something about these two that just makes you think they are going to get their shit together and do something really big.

Bonbon, Grover

American Labrador Grover married Chihuahua bitch Bonbon in a pet marriage yesterday at All Saints. The marriage was performed at a group ceremony led by Brother Pasquale of the Franciscan order.

Marriage will not be the end of freedom for Grover, a cat box forager and bomb-sniffer's apprentice. At the ceremony, he flung saliva as his massive brown head swung from stimulus to stimulus.

The irritable bride stamped the ground, whining to be picked up as her new husband ate a huge bowl of chocolate cake, vomited, and humped a child seat, his body arcing and his glistening, catsup-red manhood shimmering under the photographer's lights.

Mr. Grover's previous wife ran away.

Lydia Faber,
Dale Carr

When Dale Carr and Lydia Faber take their vows tomorrow at Pier 60, Chelsea Piers, the words "in sickness and in health" will have special meaning.

It was a hospital that brought the couple together.

Several years ago, Dale Carr, 62, was visiting a friend who was recovering from an appendectomy at NYU's Tisch Medical Center. While in the waiting room, he struck up a conversation with Emily Faber, whose grandmother, Lydia Faber, also was recovering from surgery.

"Emily was gushing about her grandmother, and by the end of our chat, I knew I would have to find a way to meet her," said Mr. Carr.

"Dale asked if I would maybe introduce him to my grandma some time, and at that very moment, Grandma walked out into the waiting room—by herself, without a wheelchair," Emily Faber recalled. "She was grinning from ear to ear."

So was Mr. Carr: Emily's grandma's surgery had been successful, her breasts enlarged from a 32-A to a 40-DD. He proposed to her at P.F. Chang's two weeks later.

Tamara Austin,
Jonathan Valnik

Tamara Austin, a real estate lawyer, was married Saturday to Jonathan Valnik, a salesman, at the St. Paul Chapel in Groton, Conn.

The bride, 27, graduated *magna cum laude* from Harvard and received her law degree from Yale, also *magna cum laude*.

The bridegroom, 33, received his B.A. from McKendrall University.

It's a small, private school in Ohio. He did get into other schools, but McKendrall's teacher-to-student ratio was really appealing. Just because you haven't heard of it doesn't mean – you know what? Fuck you.

Jane Resnick,
Paul Merrill

Jane Resnick and Paul Merrill were married yesterday at the Los Palos Community Center. A friend of the couple's, Universal Life Church Minister Tim Hoddle, performed the civil ceremony.

Ms. Resnick, 28, is the founder and proprietor of The Bead 'n' Seed store in Ukiah, CA. The store operates using a unique model of "community commerce," whereby shoppers can milk goats or provide child care in exchange for beads or seeds.

The bride's parents are Dr. and Mrs. John Resnick of Long Island. Dr. Resnick is chief of Neurosurgery at Massachusetts General Hospital.

The bridegroom, 39, is also a "doctor": "Dr. Stoopid," a noted medical marijuana advocate who passes out joints from a unicycle.

Maria Bellanesta, The Pope

Maria Bellanesta was married on Saturday to the Pope at a private ceremony that he performed.

The wedding is the first for the head of the Catholic Church, which forbids marriage for clergy. The union was annulled the next morning by the Pope himself, who issued a written mea culpa from the Vatican.

"I blew it," he said in the statement. "And Jesus knows it."

The Pope said he met Ms. Bellanesta at a bar in San Francisco during an official Church business trip. The holy father shared a bottle of sambuca with the 24-year-old fashion designer and then married her in the parking lot of a nearby gas station, CITGO.

Ms. Bellanasta said the rendezvous occurred on Halloween.

"I didn't know he was a real Pope," argued the bride. "I mean, did he think I was a real Ninja Turtle?"

...*for richer or poorer*

Today's couples want a memorable wedding that doesn't break the bank. Here are seven ways that one couple, Sam and Cindy Forsythe of Santa Fe, made their big day ...

Affordably Elegant

1 Sam and Cindy didn't hire a **professional wedding photographer**—normally a $5,000 to $10,000 expense. Instead, they hired a caricaturist from the boardwalk to make big-head drawings of each guest playing their favorite sport.

2 They saved another $2,000 by foregoing a **disc jockey or band**, instead tying pots and pans to some dogs' tails.

3 Then, instead of spending hundreds of dollars on a **horse-drawn carriage** to take them from the reception to the hotel, they *made* $800 by selling some of their old salt-water aquarium tubes.

4 In lieu of spending $400 to $500 on a **magician**, they spent $70 on a magician.

5 Queasy about splurging on a lighthouse, they had their friend Ben make a **foghorn** out of a chicken and a can of shaving cream, saving millions.

6 For the reception, they decided against roasting a pig, and opted to **warm up** a live pig and then give it back to the farmer. Cost: zero dollars.

7 Finally, instead of having sex on their wedding night, they rented the **porn**.

Total Savings:

$39,700,000

Aimee Bayley,
Tye Kerler

VOWS

ON Tye and Aimee Kerler's honeymoon, rest and relaxation were the furthest thing from their minds.

"We weren't going to miss the biggest event of the year for him," said Mrs. Kerler, 27. "Karate is his life, and the championship in Bangkok is the big enchilada."

So seven hours after the couple was married at the Pike Place Lodge in Seattle, they flew to Thailand.

But fighting was not all that they had planned.

"You'd think that karate would be enough stress," said the 29-year-old groom, who fights Tiger Style. "But to adopt a baby while we were there—it was nuts."

"It was a huge success," said Mrs. Kerler. "We've got a new kid, and Tye took second place. I'm so proud of him."

"I'm not," said the bridegroom. "Tye's not proud of Tye at all. Tye let everyone down. Second place karate trophy? Shit. That's the only trophy you get immediately after getting your ass kicked. And in front of my new little son, too. Suck."

Kaitlyn Brown, Ron Belisle

Kaitlyn Brown and Ron Belisle tied the knot at the Woodside Country Club on Friday night. The Rev. Paul James officiated.

The two met using an online dating service known as People-Meeter.com.

"We're so perfect for each other," said the bride, a hairdresser from Naples, Florida. "Ron likes books; I like books. I like beaches; he likes beaches. The computer matched us perfectly."

"It matched our traits right down the line," said the groom, also a hairdresser. "I'm just a little surprised that it paired me with a woman."

Donna Haley, Mack Johnson

Life on the road suits Mack Johnson just fine. That's why friends and family of the 28-year-old maverick were a little surprised when he told them that he was settling down, and yes, getting married.

"That ain't Mack," said the groom's father, Carter Johnson. "I don't care what you say; the road is in his blood. Before too long, he'll be back to runnin' around."

But the bride, Donna Haley, 26, disagreed: "Carter's as full of beans as a burlap sack. I know the road is in Mack's blood, but that don't mean he can't settle down."

"I hate to say it," said the bride's mother, Gladys Haley, "but I agree with Carter. Mack ain't the settlin' type. He just ain't. He's sweet as pie, but he's got the road in his blood, and once it's in there, it can't never come out—not even by a blood transfusion."

"Oh, listen to all this," said bridesmaid Fonda Charles. "Nobody's even giving them a chance. Don't people see what the power of love can do? Doesn't anyone even remember *The Titanic*? Sure Mack's got the road in his blood, but Donna's

---

> ## "... he's got the road in his blood, and once it's in there, it can't never come out—not even by a blood transfusion."

---

a strong woman—if anyone can tame that wild stallion it's her."

"We'll see," said the bride's grandmother, Clarice Haley. "He's got a wandering streak, and he's got the road in his blood, but she's strong. Only time will tell."

"Oh hell," said the bride's grandfather, Jerrold "Hi-C" Haley. "This isn't Spencer Tracy and Katharine Hepburn we're talking about here. They're just a coupla no-good software engineers."

Candice Fuentes, Richard Thielmann

Candice Fuentes and Rich Thielmann are to be married at the reception hall of the Thielmann Statistics Institute in Cupertino, Calif. on Friday. The civil ceremony will be performed by Nathan Morris.

Mr. Thielmann, 39, an actuary by training, founded his institute in 1989 to provide statistical services to governments.

"He's so smart. I love the way his mind works," said the bride, 31, a kindergarten teacher. "When he starts talking, my eyes just glaze over like a potato. It's hard to describe what I'm feeling—it's not boredom ..."

"Candice is one in a million," said the groom. "One in 7.432 million, technically: For a guy like me to end up with a girl like this would be less likely than finding an Indian arrowhead wrapped in a two-dollar bill in a garbage Dumpster each day of the week for a year. With divorce rates at 49.8%, and assuming she hates me by about 3% more each year, annualized, I have a very good chance of dying before getting divorced."

Virginia Johnson, Artemis Bold

Virginia Johnson and Artemis Bold were married on Friday at the Golden Gate Botanical Gardens in San Francisco. The ceremony was performed by Zambini the Magnificent.

The couple first met after one of the bridegroom's shows. "It was a bachelorette party for one of my friends from college," said the bride, 33, "and we thought, 'Wouldn't it be great to see something really retarded, like a magic show?' Sure enough, there's Artemis up on stage with the wand, the cape, everything."

"The mind's eye is never prepared for the power: the power of ILLUSION!" said the groom, 31. "Lest the mind be unprepared, let the magic take its course, and be prepared to TAKE YOU AWAY!"

"Yes, he always talks like that," said Ms. Johnson, who is a veterinarian. "To me, that's not magic. Magic is sewing a puppy's hand back on."

Lisa Lambe,
Joshua Hecklemin

Lisa Lambe and Joshua Hecklemin were married on Saturday evening at St. Mary of the Assumption Church in Fair Park, Ill. Father Ted Maroney performed the ceremony.

Mrs. Hecklemin is a principal at Guigal Temens, a design firm in Chicago. She graduated *summa cum laude* from Brown University, where she was the editor of the literary journal *Word/Journeys*.

The groom is some kind of finance/investment guy. Who cares. Lisa—judging by the photo alone—looks like she has that tender spark. She's 28, which means she would have graduated from Brown about seven or eight years ago, exactly when I was finishing up at Providence College.

We almost certainly crossed paths there—in a café, a bar, on the bus. My problem back then, and to some extent now, was/is confidence. Lisa and I would have connected on so many levels. I would have treated her like an angel, an angel made out of sugar.

Phyllis Baumgarten, Jim Cantrall

VOWS

The best gifts come in small packages. For Phyllis and Jim Cantrall, the small packages took the form of miniature horses.

The groom, 32, who founded the mini-horse aid organization known as Painted Promise, met Ms. Baumgarten at a mini donkey round-up for singles.

"Everyone in this community knows Phyllis," he said. "Something about small horses brings out a big heart in this girl."

The bride, 30, who maintains the website Lil' Horsehelper. com, was wooed by the groom's commitment to these animals.

"He's really been an innovator in the world of tiny equine charity," she said. "In 2007 alone, he raised $240. For animals this small, that's a huge amount of money. Remember that even a big mini-horse can be smaller than a human hair."

"Sometimes I do wonder if we're talking about the same kind of mini-horse," said the groom. "I'm thinking of the ones that are about the size of a Great Dane."

Jay Gatsby, Daisy Buchanan

VOWS

Jay Gatsby, formerly James Gatz, of West Egg, Long Island Sound, married Daisy Buchanan nee Fay, of East Egg, on Saturday at Mr. Gatsby's residence.

Mr. Gatsby is a self-made businessman said to be involved in bootlegging, though many positions have been ascribed to him, including that of European Count.

Ms. Buchanan, the former wife of Tom Buchanan the athlete, married Tom for social position after the young Gatsby, whom she loved, went off to war. She can't say she never loved Tom. She had no idea Gatsby would return and become immensely wealthy.

It looked like there might not be a happy ending for Mr. Gatsby and his bride after Ms. Buchanan accidentally hit and killed her ex-husband's mistress while driving Mr. Gatsby's coupé.

"But it all worked out!" said Mr. Gatsby. "Just like in the moving pictures."

The maid of honor was Jordan Baker, the golf champion. The best man was Nick Carraway, the bond trader.

The reception featured a lavish spread of suckling pigs nestled against turkeys and pousson, all baked an otherworldly brown, salads of Moroccan design, and gins and liquors of every variety.

For entertainment, a set of twins conducted a baby act in costume, and champagne was served in glasses as big as cereal bowls.

The wedding was attended by The Chester Beckers, the Leeches, the Blackdick Clan, a man named Klipspringer, the Hornbeams, The Count Arthur Strongs, the O.R.P. Schraeders, Admiral Gabriel Weisert, the Fishguards, a magician called Van Fabian, Mack's valet (Mr. Mikos), the Sorwell Sisters, the Fitzpiper Brothers (Shasta, Ginger and Taffy), Captain Tonsilbanger, Old Gay Greg Hogg, Schwartz's son Downshumper, Long-Tongue Davey, Karly Cotswills of Shananay, O'Hoolran the Pee Drinker, Babyhead Beaver, the young Quinns, Lambskin Lester, Loonway Gahalaha, the Hot Air Balloon Festival Flasher, Whitebait the tobacco importer, Shams of Tabriz, Ernest Lily and Emily Cat-Tits his fiancée, the Fusselbinder crew from Orchid's Hound's Balls, Miss Beverly Beeman, Crackerjack, Little Minge, Tipp Ferret, and a man everyone called Dr. Stoopid.

MODERN LOVE

The Signals Said 'Stop,'
but He Was on my 'Go' List

FROM the start, I knew everything about Jason was wrong.

I am a list maker, so I wrote out the "pros and cons." The con list was longer. It filled four jumbo index cards and a piece of butcher paper in my study: Jason was emotionally unavailable; he was married—to two other women, and living separate lives with each family in different states; he didn't like animals; or plants; he didn't know what math was, or what the colors of a traffic light meant.

I had met Jason online, and we started e-mailing. There was chemistry, even in our electronic exchanges. This is the paradox about love in the Internet age: everyone seems *Unheimliche*—familiar and unfamiliar at the same time.

We arranged a date.

In real life, Jason's dark, brooding eyes and shy smile were even more beguiling than in his picture. He introduced me to some of his biological and adopted kids: Asian, Latino, Black, and White. He had named each kid after their race.

He told me more about his past, and how he wanted to change. He begged me to give him a chance and, reluctantly, I did.

We spent Saturdays walking on the wharf. He whistled arias from my favorite operas and told me about his plans to start a non-alcoholic winery. He said he wanted to tell both of his wives about the other wife and family, and then wipe the slate clean and start anew, or maybe keep just one of the wives—the hotter, younger one.

During one of our wharf walks, Jason revealed more. "I have a lot of credit card debt," he said.

"It's OK," I told him.

"And," he said, "I was the Hot Air Balloon Festival Flasher."

I made another list, this time with Post-its. They covered up my computer screen, so that I had trouble finding the restart icon. This is love, I thought: it makes you unable to restart your computer. I laughed, thinking of Jason.

In the fall Jason invited me to his summer home in the country. He cooked me dinner. He had named each seductive course after a quality he said he admired in me ("Honesty Spinach," "Hot Meatloaf," "Breast

---

He told me about his plans to start a non-alcoholic winery.

Ice Creams," etc.).

When the cold dessert-spoon touched my lips, I felt my heart melt.

After the meal, we shared a bottle of Cidre Bouché, and my arm brushed against his. I saw all the lists I'd made. "There are so many reasons this is wrong," I told him. "But I can't help myself."

"I have something else to tell you," Jason said. I bit my lip and opened my heart. He held me tight and stuttered, "I th-think ..."

"Go on," I said. "You can say it."

"D-D-Daddy blew up the potty."

He had started a grease fire in the compost toilet. "We should g-g-get the fuck outta here," he moaned.

As we sped away, I watched Jason's cottage burn in the rearview mirror of his scooter. I thought of all the memories that would be engulfed in those flames. I also wondered if the fire might be a way for Jason to free himself from his past as we embarked on a new future together.

"I'm sorry about your house," I shouted at him through the night wind, but secretly I was happy for the delicious symbolism.

"It's OK!" Jason said. "That wasn't my house! I found it while I was hiking and it was basically unlocked!"

I squeezed his waist and cried. I felt joy. A stream of mucus trailed from my nose and danced in the wind like a Tibetan prayer flag.

Here we are, I thought, me and my Magic Man, speeding through a red light down the dark highway of love.

Sharon Bassinger is a writer living in Brooklyn. Her novel, And We Prayed in the Supermarket of the Divine, *will be published by Mortar and Pestle Press in July.*

Bunny Peters,
Jason Carlisle

Bunny Peters and Jason Carlisle were married yesterday on the Quack Attack, an amphibious party boat in San Diego, California. Captain Richard Pound presided.

The bride, 21, is a "lights-out drinker" from San Diego State University.

The bridegroom, 22, is a "sloppy drunk." Too intoxicated to say "I do," he instead repeatedly screamed, "More cowbell!"

The couple is honeymooning at the Serenity Puma Rehab Ranch in El Tejon.

Ellen Hollisberry, Drake Winger

Ellen Hollisberry and Drake Winger were married on Saturday at the Playa Conoces in Baja, Mexico.

The ceremony, which was performed by the Reverend Terry Summerwell, took place on the beach at sunset.

No guests attended.

"We sent out the invitations and everything," said the bridegroom, "but I guess people were too busy."

"It was a destination wedding," said the bride, "which automatically affects the numbers right there."

"I guess that is a new wedding record," said the bridegroom. "Zero guests."

"I've seen an eight-guest wedding, saw a three-guest wedding once, even saw a one-guest wedding," said Rev. Summerwell. "But you gotta be a serious piece of driftwood to pull off a zero-guest wedding. Amen. My hat's off to them."

Gabrielle Nordecchio, Richard Larna

VOWS

Gabrielle Nordecchio and Richard Larna were married on Friday at the Polish Hall in Brooklyn, New York. Friends, family, and luminaries of the New York art world were in attendance.

Mr. Larna, 54, is a painter who rose meteorically within the Brooklyn Post-Nemendamist movement in the 1970s.

"Art is a cuckoo business," said the bridegroom. "One day they love you, the next day you're crap. But this last review really blindsided me."

The review, which appeared in the Spring issue of *Ointment*, was written by his now-wife, Ms. Nordecchio, an art critic. It was published one day after the couple's wedding ceremony.

"I had to be honest," said the bride, 48. "I can't water down my work just because I'm married to him."

Her article was called "Castle Stupid Has a New King, and his Name is Dick Larna."

"We're going to get past this," said Ms. Nordecchio, who

> ## "Art is a cuckoo business. One day they love you, the next day you're crap."

will be keeping her name. "He's a painter. I'm a critic. We're both just doing our jobs."

"Yeah. Maybe Gabrielle will like my next painting better," Mr. Larna said. "It's going to be called, 'The Artist's Ex-wife and her Bitch-Ass Ferret.'"

Helen Ing,
Joseph Abeya

Dr. Joseph Abeya and Helen Ing were married yesterday. The ceremony was performed at the New York State Prison at Attica by the Rev. Sgt. Tom Dwyer.

Ms. Ing, who will keep her name, is the daughter of Donald and Su-Li Ing of Forest Glen, Michigan. Her father is the retired owner of the Hong Kong Pacific Trading Company. Her mother is an organizer for the Chinese-American coalition in Dearborn, Michigan.

Dr. Abeya is a resident in nephrology at SUNY, Buffalo. He is the son of the late Dr. Marcus Abeya and Mrs. Louise Kim Abeya of Scranton, Pa. His mother works for the Scranton Realty Group.

Ms. Ing is a spy for China and she will be executed on Friday at the New York State Prison at Attica.

Cindy Cornwall, Barry Hofstetter

Cindy Cornwall and Barry Hofstetter were married Saturday at the Chapel of the Bells in Las Vegas, Nevada.

Ms. Cornwall is a dancer. Mr. Hofstetter is a blackjack dealer. That's probably enough column space for these two.

Martania Progryov, Margeb Hygrsky

Martania Progryov and Margeb Hygrsky is getting married last Tuesday. The ceremony was carried out by Hon. Ted B. Johnson, justice of the supreme court of little state named Rhode Island but is not actual island.

Mrs. Progryov is currently a candidate of Online Masters in the history of Pilgrims at the university of New York of Ohio. He studies so hard the very first thanksgiving including where did the Mayflower come from? And why is it turkey that they eat with savages that first time? She meet her new mate at watering hole called Hog Pit where many people goes for getting sex.

He, on the other hand, is Mr. Hygrsky. A remarkable father of five in the future if he can help it. He would like that, to be in the garage making projects probably, you bet. Fertility is Martania's number one thing.

The bride and groom herself which was joined by much of the family and the friends having honeymoon of you guessed it: the waterfalls of Niagara!

Sylvia Dinella, Gus Fox

Sylvia Dinella married Gus Fox on Saturday at the Kalama Community center in Kalama, Wash. The spiritual advisor Jade Harper officiated.

Mr. Fox, 48, is a logger in the Cascade Mountains. The couple met when he felled an 80-year-old ponderosa pine tree with a chainsaw.

When the tree toppled, Ms. Dinella's head was poking up from the hollow stump.

"I guess she is a tree nymph or a tree creature," said Mr. Fox. "Honestly, it's just something we've never talked about."

McKenzie Hess, Sandeep Rao

VOWS

When McKenzie Hess and Sandeep Rao started dating, they discovered that the best way to keep in touch—and madly in love—during their busy days was to send text messages to each other. They are part of a new generation of romantic texters, or "heterotextuals."

"Texting may seem really modern, but it is a way of going back to the written form of romance," observed the bridegroom. "One of the benefits is that you can look at it later and remember what it was like—just like our grandparents did with their stack of love letters."

The couple's first text was simple and innocent enough:

> "Hey U"
> "watcha doin?"
> "sitng in mtng"
> "oop. Srry :)"

After a week, the following exchange took place:

"Hey bb"
"watcha doin"
"going 2 gym"
"don't get 2 buff, yer my emo boy"
"K shug, don't get 2 hot"

After six months, the messages became even more intimate:

"hey"
"watcha doin?"
"Jst hangin with sum dudz"
"want 2 get with me? ;)"
"L8er 4 sure; wen I'm dun here, yah"
"K"

Now, after two years together, on the eve of their wedding, this Saturday at Memphis City Hall, the messages show familiarity, fondness, and all of the hectic energy that weddings bring:

"Hey"
"wutz up?"
"@ the cake place with deposit"
"erm I paid that"
"???"
"can U pik up flwers pleez :)"
"whre the fk R they"
"R U mad?"
"where"
"@ city center. luv U bb."

The bride's response was a modern classic. "K," she texted.

Best Sellers

Books for BRIDES-to-Be

1

1,785

JENNY'S WEDDING,
by Milosz Hosled
When a woman attempts to remodel
her vacation home in Tuscany, an
old demon returns. She struggles
to overcome her tongue-rolling
compulsion in time to marry
a veterinarian.

---

2 **EVE'S WOMB: HEALTHY WEDDING RECIPES FOR THE ORGANIC AGE,** 408
by Patty Baker with Susan Chase-Springer.
Fibrous recipes, including Granola Grundies, Millet Cake Bowl, and
Grass-Fed Sprue.

---

3 **PRINCESS, HOBBIT, TERRORIST,** *by Sheila Buress.* 3
Author argues that ring-bearers and flower girls are "attention
vampires" who ruin half to a third of all weddings.

---

4 **MY PERFECT DAY: A BRIDE'S GUIDE TO DIVORCE,** *by Tricia Bowles.* 1
Tips for the other big day, from pantsuits to no-smear eyeliner.

---

5 **A POT TO PISS IN,** *by Claire Billings with Lisa Monette.* 62
Planning the perfect budget wedding.

---

6 **IS HE IN MY SAME CHAKTI? THE MANUAL OF SPIRITUAL** 899
COMPATIBILITY, *by Heather Rodgers.* A guide to finding the right
man, using star mapping, energy charts, and by flipping bramanaputi
nuggets.

Jacqueline Butler, Jeff Corton

Jacqueline Butler and Jeff Corton were married on Saturday in Denver, Co. at Central Baptist Church. Reverend Dan Staples performed the ceremony.

The bride and groom, both 38, met at Dr. Wayne Leopold's "You Can Have Much, Much More Love" workshop in nearby Ridgeway.

The system focuses on identifying obstacles to love caused by "Intimacy Vampires" and "Emotional Garbage People."

"My ex, Deanna, turned out to be an Intimacy Vampire," said the groom, "and my brother Bill, too. I'm glad those two are together now, so they can suck each other's emotions out."

"Jeff had a lot of anger," said the bride. "That's why the system was so good for both of us. I learned that my golden retriever, Hecuba, was an Emotional Garbage Person. As soon as I gave him to a farmer, I shot up to Level 4 on the Groswer Slice."

The couple plan to spend their honeymoon at Dr. Leopold's national workshop.

"We want to finish the entire program," said the groom, "get the yellow suits, meet up with the mother ship, the whole nine yards."

Purple Delicious, Marmot

Purple Delicious married Marmot at Green Creek Organic Farms in Chemeketa, Ca. on Friday.

Purple Delicious, 26, born Eileen Vincent Beckman, is the daughter of Danielle and Vincent Beckman, founders of Beckman Aerospace and Defense International.

"We're not proud of where our parents' money came from," said the bride. "Marmot and I have cut ourselves off from that, totally, except for just enough to follow the String Cheese Incident and run my little ocarina business."

"Now we want to give some of that blood money back to the people who have been hurt by it," said the bridegroom, 27, formerly Dennis Northrop-Grumman, "in the form of a cool adobe home for us with solar panels and stuff."

"And a huge playhouse for Bree and Raven," added the bride.

"The wedding was carbon neutral," said the bridegroom, "except for the cupcakes. All of the other reception foods were made from locally grown produce. It was so special to both Purple and me to be able to provide from the earth's womb: I think all of the barfing was just people releasing toxins they brought from the city."

The Fayre Gwyneth, Rozner the Warrior

VOWS

Joeity and gayness rayned down on the merry-makers yester's eve in the glen, a solemn nimbus parting, an omen— a rainbow—and y-gad!—a clap of thunder—then exploding doves did trumpet and signal the nuptials. Rozner, the stee-ley-eyed groom, of hard heart here melted. Gwyneth, fayre dame, silken braids kist against apple cheeks, and her flanking cherub maids envy the bride her imminent flowering.

A-feasting and elation follow, with mead rivers and mounded legs of fowl festooning the banquet herd. A glint in Rozner's eye as he stomps a jig and elbows, aye, his loyal fellows.

Now the decorous dance joins groom with mother of the

feal bride, twice in years as her daughter but doubly fayre, and Rozner bulges from his loin-skirts as they step the ceremonious pattern. Fruhilde, whose fleshy gates did usher forth sweet Gwyneth, stares simmeringly at the barn-boy-cum-squire that will nigh plow her youngest's plush terroir.

Weighed with shame his man-chimes clang—kaloy!— against the saddle ...

The clock's hand's turn past midnight, and—lo!—the haze of mead blinds good Rozner and confounds him in a moral mayze. Pink dagger drawn, the valiant warrior plunges into the birth-swamp that bore his wife to be, commands the princely penaz into the Nile of his mother-in-law's hungry hollow sheath.

Shame! Eternal shame to Rozner as the dawn breaks over the debauch-ed feast. The once-proud warrior surveys his nuptial bed bereft of true bride, and the marital sheets a-mess with Fruhilde and beflecked with passion's pre-dewdrops.

The hero's brow is strafed with sorrow as he hops upon his swayback steed. Weighed with shame his man-chymes clang—kaloy!—against the saddle, and his heart pounds heavy in his chest.

To the East he sails, seeks refuge from his sullied past. And there he spends his days a-beggar'd and alone. He is solitary, save the sweet honey of the dames de japonais. And the hungry chinois and the greedy mouths of Malays, the only comfort for his sorrow.

Bernice Bannister, Stephen Shipley

Bernice Eleanor Bannister and Stephen Lee Shipley were married on Saturday by the Reverend Pace Newfeld at the Hapsbury Farm near Nashua, New Hampshire.

The bride, 35, runs a rabbit rescue and rehabilitation center in Nashua. The groom, 38, is a doctoral candidate in Geology at the University of New Hampshire. He is also a part-time falconer.

In separate attempts to surprise one another, both Ms. Bannister and Mr. Shipley released groups of their respective hobby animals into a nearby pasture: she, a warren of Dutch lops; he, a cauldron of Peregrine falcons.

Ms. Bannister said the ensuing massacre, "undid years of my work."

Mr. Shipley said, "Nature is not sentimental. But I am sorry that the birds did not obey my recall phrase, 'Hilo, ho, boys, come birds, come.'"

"That's not what he yelled," said the bride's sister. "He yelled, 'Mommy! Bunny! No!'"

Clarice Mackey, Randall Jones

Clarice Mackey and Randall Jones were married at the Albuquerque City Hall on Friday. The ceremony was performed by Deputy Clerk Herman Grayson.

"This is the beginning of a very interesting journey for us," said Ms. Mackey, 30.

"We're always going to be learning new things about each other," said Mr. Jones, 40. "I think that's what she means."

"Like I just learned that he wasn't ever in the Marines," said the bride. "He was actually in an *a cappella* singing group called The Maureens."

"The two lead singers were named Maureen," countered the groom, "and we did tour Vietnam. It was no cake walk."

Mary and James Florian

STATE OF THE UNION

Not every marriage has the unanimous blessings of friends and family.

When Mary Heppner and James Florian were married last year at the Hafferty Club near Great Falls, Mt., some of the bridegroom's circle were slow to accept his fiancée. They were worried that the groom's inheritance of the Florian Furniture fortune played a part in her desire to marry him.

All is calm now, on their first anniversary, but their wedding was not immune to these apprehensions. The groomsmen protested with golden armbands to symbolize "gold digger," and at the rehearsal dinner the groom's grandmother gave a toast that began, "Mary, one thing about marrying for money is that you earn every penny."

Even the officiant, Father Tom Boonan, paused and looked

"... one thing about marrying for money is that you earn every penny ..."

---

at the bride for an uncomfortable beat after saying the line "for richer or for poorer." At that moment, recalled the guests, the bride diffused the tension with a well-timed joke when she asked, "What are my choices again?"

"They were just being protective of their friend and family member," recalled Mrs. Florian. "I understand, but they have nothing to worry about. I would have married James if he were worth half what he is. I just don't want to live like some animal with a time card and a bus pass."

Caroline Pilliner, Marshall Ditus III

Caroline Pilliner and Marshall Ditus III were married yesterday on the trading floor of the New York Stock Exchange.

The bride, 31, is a Senior Vice President of TYHR-MereCom, a company that helps yacht owners maximize returns on their docking investments by renting timeshares for empty berths.

The bridegroom, 35, is managing partner at Capital Stream, an investment conglomerate that buys rivers from developing countries.

At the wedding rehearsal dinner, guests were invited to eat diamonds out of a heap of Beluga feces.

It is with great sadness that Mr. and Mrs. Paul Simmons announce the marriage of their daughter

Jennifer Simmons
to
Tom Francis

on Thursday
the Twenty Second of May
at Three O'Clock
at St. Christopher's Church
in Plainview, Minnesota

"And [Jenny] did settle for an unworthy husband during that man-famine, and his fanciful stories and plans did spray forth upon her family ..."

—Ezekiel 4:12

Claire Sapolski, Glen Ferrell

Claire Sapolski and Glen Ferrell were married at Highgate Tea Gardens in London on Saturday. The Rev. Morton Paisley presided.

"She's a right brick," said the groom, 28. "To say I'm enamored of her is a bloody understatement."

"Indeed," said the bride, 24. "I'm unspeakably fond of Glen. He's a chum."

"I don't know why they talk like that," said the bride's mother, Doris Sapolski. "They're both from New Jersey. I know they loved their trip to England, but they sound like damn C3PO."

"They sound like Hannibal Lecter," said the bride's father, Charles Sapolski.

"Ooh, he was the worst," added Mrs. Sapolski. "He'd kill anything that moved. All he wanted to do was kill people and eat them."

Annie Hansen, Trevor Guillen

Annie Hansen and Trevor Guillen were married on Sunday at the Sandstone Chapel in Sea Side, Va.

Mr. Guillen and Ms. Hansen met at a restaurant near the business park where both are employed, but Ms. Hansen admitted she had seen him before.

According to the bride, 27, "everyone in town" recognizes Mr. Guillen, 29, who is the star of one of the most-watched videos in Internet history.

"It was totally unexpected, but being an Internet phenom is cool," said the bridegroom. "I wish it had been for something else, like my guitar playing, but hey, fame is fame."

The video, entitled "security guard sets his own nuts on fire," has been watched more than two billion times.

Eva Robertson, Jason Compson, Jr.

VOWS

Eva Mary Robertson, 23, and Jason Compson, Jr., 43, were married Saturday at the Redeemer Baptist Church in the town of Jefferson in Yoknapatawpha County, Mississippi.

Mr. Compson is the son of Mr. and Mrs. Jason Compson, Sr. The bridegroom resides in the family home with his ailing mother, two house servants named Dilsey and Luster, his mentally challenged brother Benjy, and the child of the incestuous union of his sister Caddy and brother Quentin, the latter now deceased. He supports them all by working at a store in town.

"... I aint one of these hayseeds thinks hes going to get a mountain of gold ..."

"I got no problem with no good honest whore," he said. "Better than all these folks tell you one thing and mean another like Earl who hasn't got enough to do besides selling a nickels worth of nails to some country farmer that he cant keep out of another mans business, I says to him Ill trade places with you any day because it takes a man like me not to have anymore sense than to pay some Eastern Jew broker to lose my money. But I aint one of these hayseeds thinks hes going to get a mountain of gold from the corn market when the manipulators have the inside track. As soon as I get even Im done with it for good and that oughta please this house full of no good servants, one idiot, and a little slut of a girl whose food I put on the table every day without so much as a thank you Jason."

Ms. Robertson, daughter of Jarrell and Judith Roberston, is an Internet marketing consultant with Go Up! Corporation.

Emily Weaver, Gregory Ash

Emily Diane Weaver married Gregory Jerrold Ash on Del Dueno Beach at the Golf Resort in Palm Beach, Florida.

The bride, 34, is a dentist at Horton Hears a Smile in Sarasota. Her father, Dr. Stan Weaver, is also a dentist, retired after 45 years in private practice. The bride's mother, Dr. Courtney Weaver, is also a retired dentist.

The groom, 35, is real estate agent with Marallay Properties.

"Sure they're smart, and I respect what they do," said the groom, "but I think I know my own mouth better than anyone. I'm gonna keep doing my own dentistry."

Elizabeth Freccero,
Neil Reynolds

Elizabeth Freccero and Neil Reynolds were married on Saturday at a church in the USA.

The ceremony was performed by Mr. Joseph Daniel, the FOREIGN AFFAIRS DIRECTOR OF NIGERIA who is in need of your most esteemed assistance in this very confidential affair.

Mr. Daniel is in possession of the sum of $1,000,000,38474 millions and with your utmost trust and help must ask your assistance in getting it safely out of the country. HIS DOCTOR TOLD HIM THAT HE WOULD NOT EXCEED MORE THAN FIVE MORE MONTHS DUE TO CANCER PROBLEM OF THE PEDUNDULAM AND THORAT. THE ONE THAT DISTURBS HIM MOST IS HIS BLOOD PRESSURE SICKNESS. HIS WIFE IS A JUNIOR PRINCESS (PRINCESS ROSEMARY KHALIFA), TOO YOUNG TO ACCEPT THE FUNDS.

If you are interested, the Mr. Jeff Daniels is ready to pay 10% interest of one million thousand hundred. Please send your kind and urgent response to Mr. Daniel.

You and God and I are a threesome,
Mr. Joseph Daniel

Joanne and Mitch Tilson in 1973.

YESTERDAY AND TODAY

Joanne and Mitch Tilson

Joanne Tilson remembers seeing her husband, Mitch, for the first time 43 years ago, near the main quad at Berkeley.

"He was gorgeous. He had these long curly locks and he was so strong, like Samson," she said. "They were protesting a wage freeze imposed on the city's mostly black sanitation workers."

"We were each sitting inside our own garbage can," remembers Mr. Tilson, "wearing black face, and chanting 'white man's wages for ne-gro gar-bage men!' Everyone thought it was pretty cool, and they ended up getting a two cent pay hike."

The pair began dating and were married that summer, when Mrs. Tilson was four months pregnant.

"I figured, 'Let's do this now before I start showing,'" she

"Back then, you could have a drink or a couple of 'ludes during pregnancy..."

said. "I decided I'd rather have morning sickness at my wedding than wear a maternity dress!"

"Back then, you could have a drink or a couple of 'ludes during pregnancy," said Mrs. Tilson. "So Mikeela, our firstborn, has kind of a wolf snout.

"Those were the times," laughed Mrs. Tilson. "We were the quintessential California couple. Mitchell even got drafted."

"Yep, cut my pinky off with a fingernail clipper," he said. "That settled that. Did the civil rights thing, moved to Marin."

"Had eight more children. Became a real estate agent," Mrs. Tilson said. "Got into coke in the eighties. Had a big house fire."

And what do they wish they had done differently?

"I wish I'd been born in the 14th century," said Mr. Tilson, "as far from the 60s as possible. All of the sexual freedom but none of the social responsibility."

"Definitely," said Mrs. Tilson, "I'd like to live in the future on a spaceboat or in the present, on a houseboat."

Honeymoon
Hideaways

The wedding's over. Now what? Here's a look at the pros and cons of some of the hottest honeymoon destinations around the world!

1 **Yip, South Pacific**. *The Good*: Powdered-sugar beaches, fresh fish, spectacular diving. *The Bad*: Overrun by the Habu, a murderous snake.

2 **Kennicksport Cove, Massachussets**. *The Good*: Lobster and blueberry pie, calm surf, rich whaling history. *The Bad*: Surly boatswains will try to "Queequeg" their way into your bedroll.

3 **Punta Piñajuel, Guatemala**. *The Good*: Inexpensive, colorful art, beautiful native music. *The Bad*: The cocaine is too strong for most people's taste.

4 **Largünsdøtter, Iceland**. *The Good*: Stunning natural features, friendly people, rich in tradition. *The Bad*: They treat their reindeer like dogs.

5 **Lac du Fromage, France**. *The Good*: Great wines, stunning antiques, and world-class art. *The Bad*: French farm girls will chew through your radiator hoses.

6 **Jao Torinho, Brazil.** *The Good*: Festive culture, sizzling beach scene, dancing capital of the world. *The Bad*: Sequin-thonged natives may derail your sexual orientation.

7 **Old Henry's Town, Jamaica.** *The Good*: Friendly, laid-back culture, great history, spicy cuisine. *The Bad*: Maritime museum doesn't open till 10 a.m.

8 **Top of The World State Park, Utah.** *The Good*: One of the world's natural wonders, outdoor sports mecca, budget lodges. *The Bad*: Because of nearby cult, no soda/tampons at local stores.

9 **Ogunala Preserve, Florida.** *The Good*: Pristine nature preserve, superb bird-watching, a short drive to Miami Beach. *The Bad*: Seminoles say there's a skunk-ape in the wash, moaning and emitting his Sasquatch stench.

10 **Green Hill, Oregon.** *The Good*: Gold prospecting, old growth forests, progressive culture. *The Bad*: Beaver state, so you have to lock up your wood in the car.

Anne Thompson, Trey Michener

Anne Thompson and Trey Michener are to be married on Saturday at the Point Reyes Chapel in Point Reyes, Ca.

Ms. Thompson, 36, is a locomotive engineer for the Burlington Northern Railroad and one of the first women to be an operator within the company's new electro-diesel fleet.

Mr. Michener, 37, is secretary of Hey Good Buddy's Model Railroading Club, where he leads tours, operates model trains, and oversees painting of miniature plastic figurines.

"It's so nice to have someone who shares my interests," said the bride. "Someone in the same field."

"She's out there driving a 200-ton diesel engine and I'm driving an 8-inch-long replica of that," said the bridegroom. "I support her, but I have to admit: sometimes, deep down, I want her to quit and start driving an even smaller train than me. Sometimes I feel so small that I want her to drive the tiniest fuckin' locomotive there is."

Marina Townsend
D.T. Melbeau

Marina Townsend married D.T. Melbeau yesterday at the Grand Hyatt in Grand Rapids, Mich. Their friend, Doug Blyer, a minister with the Universal Life Church, performed the ceremony.

The bride, 28, is the daughter of Josephine Leland Townsend and Theodore Townsend of Menlo Park, N.J.

The bridegroom, 29, is the son of Leslie Bowers-Kale and Neil Miller-Miller. He created his last name, Melbeau, by combining the first letter of his father's last name with two letters from his mother's last name, and a bunch of other letters, and mixing them together.

He picked his own first name, Damfeer Toadus, when he left home to attend Shit State.

Deborah Steinmetz, Kyle Baker

Deborah Steinmetz married Kyle Baker in a private ceremony on the bluffs in Moss Beach, Ca. The ceremony was performed by Leonard Coates, a minister of the Universal Life Church.

The bride, 52, flies United, and has Premiere Executive status. She is also a Gold Member with the Star Alliance. She will be keeping her name.

The bridegroom, 55, has a United Mileage Plus account, but prefers American Airlines, where he has AAdvantage Elite Status.

Ms. Steinmetz's parents, Jackie Lynn Steinmetz and George Steinmetz, also fly United, although they have never achieved Premiere Status.

Mr. Baker's parents, Linda and Doug Baker, are Mile High Club members on the Fung Wah Bus.

Holly Pritchard, David Belzam

VOWS

HOLLY Pritchard and David Belzam met on the Internet, but it took months of e-mails and phone calls before they met in person.

When they finally did, it was at the Fairview City Park in Fort Wayne, Indiana. The two hit it off and decided to get breakfast at a nearby café. The bride said the conversation just flowed, "like we had known each other our whole lives."

At the diner that morning, Mrs. Pritchard recalled, "David told me he couldn't stop looking at my eyes because he couldn't believe how green they were."

Mrs. Pritchard said she was embarrassed to tell Mr. Belzam that green was not in fact their natural color. But later in the morning, she decided to open up to him. "Dave! These aren't my real eyeballs!" she said. "My old eyes are somewhere else, along with my dick, my scooter, and my old personality. I'm starting fresh, with you. I love you!"

Jenny Chambers,
Todd Borjona

Jenny Chambers and Todd Borjona were married last Saturday at Alt 9 in New York, N.Y. Trumpeter Cyrus James performed the ceremony.

Ms. Chambers, 49, is a jazz singer whose soulful and creamy voice has graced albums by the Chauncey Brothers and guitarist Jeremy Arealoious.

Mr. Borjona, 53, is also a jazz musician. He plays the saxophone, primarily the alto. His solo album, "Groupin' With Her Majesty's Good Ship Harmony," is slated for release in June or September.

The couple's numerous other credits include the songs "Sophisticated Mannerisms"; "If I Could Flip You in Time";

"In Strode Mickey"; "I Remember Jumilla's Surgery"; "Meter Maids and Meter Misters"; "Canalope, Can a Life"; "Sometimes, Somewhere, Somebody Gotta 279291199!"; "The Sweexer Sessions"; "Just a Minute, Pompiloo"; and "How Much a Penny Was Worth If I Loved You Too Hard."

"We jammed for nine hours, with cats on bongos and a cat playing the tambourine..."

"There was so much talent at this celebration, we felt blessed, man," said the bridegroom. "We jammed for nine solid hours, with cats on bongos and a cat playing the tambourine, man, it was hip; no sheet music, no regular tunings, just really random noodling. It was epic."

Bathroom Woman, Bathroom Man

The man and the woman from the bathroom door married each other on Saturday at Telco Park.

For the ceremony, the bride and groom chose a clean, modern look.

The groom wore a pearl-colored Nehru tuxedo with matching cashmere stump-covers.

The bride wore a neck-less ivory A-line dress that accentuated her chewable-Vitamin-C-shaped head and Fun-Dip legs.

For their honeymoon, the couple is planning to mail themselves to Belize.

Maura Broderick, Thomas Coats

Maura Broderick and Thomas Coats were married yesterday at the Greenpoint Yacht Club in Washington, D.C.

The couple met at a diner near Mr. Coats' home.

The bride, 33, is executive director of Citizens for Ethics and Responsibility, a government watchdog group.

The bridegroom, 27, is the founder of Hairy Situations, an actual watchdog group.

Christy Tate,
Thomas Jones

Christy Tate and Thomas Jones are to be married this evening in Bradford, Va.

The bride, 45, is a marine mammal biologist and seal trainer at Virginia's Marine Experience Park. She holds a Master's in biology from London University.

The bridegroom, 50, is a founder of Risk Abatement Solutions, an insurance underwriting firm. He is a graduate of Williams College, where he also received a Master's degree.

The bridegroom suffers from pinnipedophilia, a pathological attraction to seals, walruses, and sea lions, and is therefore not allowed near the bride's workplace.

"Those creatures are so perfect," said the bridegroom. "But the judge said it's a no-no to party with them."

Annabelle Davis,
Charles Anderson

Annabelle Davis and Charles Anderson were married on Thursday at the Olympic Champion's Club in Carlsbad, N.M.

Ms. Davis, 28, is a professional ice skater who won the Olympic Gold Medal in Turin in 2006. She is a graduate of the Colorado School of Mines. She's also a miner—a professional coal-miner—who won the Gold Medal of Mining at Banff in 1997. As a direct descendent of Christopher Jones, the captain of the Mayflower, she is a member of the Mayflower Society and a licensed ship's captain who has won many gold medals for her excellent piloting and discovery of numerous continents. She can also build ships by herself.

Mr. Anderson, 31, has 12 black belts in every discipline of Karate which he employs to defend UN Peacekeepers and Nobel laureates. He is licensed to zoo-keep, and he can hold his breath for 10 hours. He doesn't need to ever hold his breath because he's so excellent at SCUBA. He turned down the Nobel Prize five times but decided to accept the Nobel Prize in Karate. He is an expert in race-horsing. He donated his Miata to the boy in the bubble.

The couple will be honeymooning on the space station with the President of the Harlem Globetrotters.

Melanie Parker, Stephen Winnole

Melanie Parker, daughter of Alice and Jerry Parker of North Glen, N.J., was married yesterday to Stephen Winnole at the Sunny Glen Cathedral in Farro, Md.

Ms. Parker, 31, is a project manager at Myello Communications, a public relations and special events firm in New York, where she oversees account development.

She is also currently managing business strategy meetings while the operations officer is out on maternity leave. Because of this double duty, the bride-to-be has had to minimize her involvement in creative development, an area in which she had played a crucial (if unofficial) role.

Without Ms. Parker's input, the artistic team has slowed their productivity considerably, which reverberates throughout the organization and ironically impacts her pro-tem role in operations.

Without Ms. Parker's input, the artistic team has slowed their productivity ...

The organization is also being bogged down by "blamestorming" over systems failure and data-availability issues. The bride is not an IT administrator but has been forced to "step up to the plate" in an organization that prides itself on its "liquid" skill-swapping platform.

Most of the company's core-competency team leaders are out the door at 4:59 sharp but still find time to IM their colleagues throughout the workday with links to a viral video of a panda bear sneezing.

Artwork by James Yamasaki

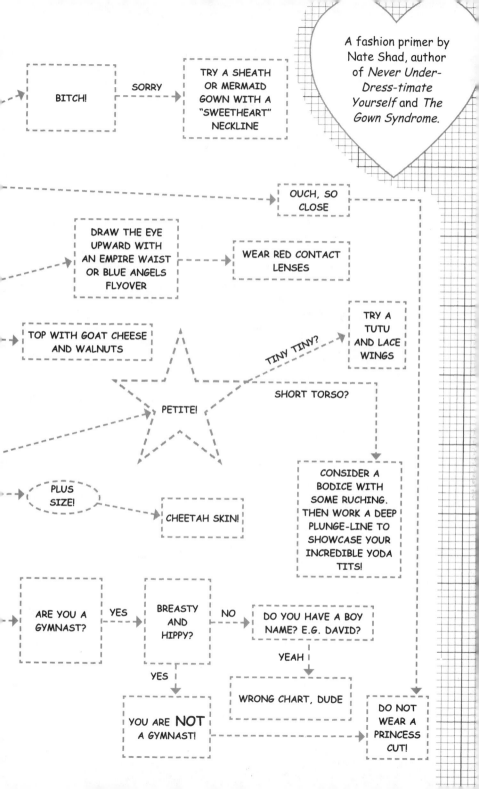

Abigail Crawford,
Lewis DeShields

Abigail Crawford married Lewis DeShields yesterday at the Women's Center Pavillion in Santa Barbara, Calif. Judge Carter Crawford, the father of the bride, officiated.

Ms. Crawford, 25, will keep her name. She works as a clerk in her father's court.

Mr. DeShields, 30, is an aphorist. His pithy sentences (including "It's better to know what you want than to be wanted, you know" and "It's better to live in trash and leisure than to be a living national treasure") have been printed in the *Santa Barbara Observer*, a weekly free ad sheet.

"Lewis can say so much by using so many less words than other people like me, or how other people would choose to say it," said the bride. "Daddy loves him."

"Love is a Stone Age currency in a high tech marketplace," he responded. "Ooh. I gotta make a mental note to write that down."

Marta Munoz,
Tyson Collins

Tyson Collins and Marta Munoz were married last week at the Two Leaves Yoga Studio in San Anselmo, Calif. Yoga Instructor Brian T. performed the ceremony.

Brian T., who teaches Rejuvenation Yoga on Thursday afternoons, Hot Yoga for Hot Singles on Friday nights, and the regular advanced Hatha classes on Mondays, Wednesdays, and Saturdays, led the guests through an invigorating, beginners-included set of poses, starting with Sukasana (seagull pose), proceeding to Matsayasana (terrier pose), and ending on a relaxing and tranquility-inducing Chaturanga Dandasana (inverted corn snake).

"It was a beautiful ceremony," said the bride's sister. "When Brian T. led us through the meditative breathing exercises, I felt two gallons of energy just shoot out my back."

Jade Kelly,
Gregory Pasternak

Jade Marie Kelly and Gregory Dale Pasternak were married on Saturday at the Municipal Picnic House in Brodeen, Wis.

Mr. Pasternak, 39, is editor in chief of "Multiple Bull-gasm: A Newsletter for the Bulldog Breeder" which he founded in 1995 while recovering from a Jet Skiing accident that was not his fault. He said the newsletter is his baby, his lover, and his goldmine.

Ms. Kelly, 34, has been deputy editor of "Multiple Bull-gasm" since 1999, when she left eFrenchie-G-Spot.biz, which folded when a factual error in one of her stories crashed the black-masked French bulldog market in Boise.

Mr. Pasternak and Ms. Kelly met when he contacted her to breed his stud, Grand National World Champion Futrell's Mr. Grumpus le Moutard, with Ms. Kelly's Open Bitch Class Champion, Happypaws' Triple Stuffed Oreo of Beckfrist.

America's Wedding Experts Offer Quick Fixes for Common

Wedding Disasters

Crisis: A puppy eats the butt out of the bridal gown.

Sarah Plover, fashion buyer for Petro Vagni:
This actually happens a lot because puppy season is also wedding season, and people want puppies at their wedding. There is a simple solution: pack wet toilet paper into the bite holes; when it dries, sew it up, corset-style, with some silk lace. It's kind of a fun, slutty Madonna look.

Crisis: The Plague

Kristin Huff, M.D., author, Ding! Dong! The Wedding's ON!:
Oh No! Buboes! Here's how to quickly deal with the crisis and get on with the wedding: Develop a volunteer system for the removal of the sick and dead to a central building, like a rectory; quickly cut up the bouquets and have guests place the petals in their pockets; break out the cigars early, even for children; and make a fun, festive 10-foot-high wall to block the death winds blowing in from Marseilles. Coughers should be dumped in the moat. Stay positive and relax. Remember, you're supposed to enjoy this!

Crisis: Gays are dominating the karaoke machine

Karen Van Buren, event planner, Germin8!:
Karaoke is a fun, spicy addition to any wedding, but it can be mobbed by the gays, who often give professional-sounding performances. Who wants to follow that? Relax: Homosexuals may be intimidating, but they are usually reasonable. Approach one of them cautiously and ask if some straight people can have a turn. Try it, and I think you will be pleasantly surprised.

Crisis: Right before the ceremony, the groom discovers that his tux bag contains a panda costume.

Jason Gruen, haberdasher at New York's Petit O$_2$:
This is a common mix-up for obvious reasons. Be calm. If there is a groomsman who shares the groom's build, use his tux. Otherwise, turn the panda suit inside out, take in the back with pins, cut off the paws, and put a jacket over it. Nobody will know it's not a tux. And you can use the panda head as a barf bin or a cool beef smoker!

Crisis: Bride's father is "a-rippin' and a-runnin.'"

Joanie Horvath, wedding planner for Memphis Magnolia:
At rural weddings, the bride's father shows up tweaked on crank just in time for the magic moment. He may take his shirt off and do martial arts, "root" people's cars, or trip out on guns or lawnmowers. Thank God there is an old Southern cure for this: an ounce of bourbon for every hour he's been awake. Remember: it's dad's special day, too. Have a great wedding!

Crisis: The officiant has the bends.

Rachel Jones-Potter, consultant, Wedding Overboard!, LLC:
It's an island wedding, and the officiant is hunched over in pain from gas bubbles in his blood. Not to fear: look for a wedding guest with an oxygen tank (hint: grandma?). Open the valve all the way and snake the thin cannula past the preacher's nasopharynx and into the trachea. Voila: you've just bought yourself four more hours. Mahalo!

Crisis: The word "WHORE!!" is scrawled across the cake in giant, red frosting letters.

Marci Rodd, pastry chef at Bistro Pol Pot, Los Angeles:
Every bride wants things to be perfect on her wedding day, but sometimes the people at the bakery can make embarrassing mistakes with icing messages. Take a deep breath. With red lipstick and a butter knife you can edit your own cake on the fly. "WHORE" can easily become "W$_e$HOPE You Like the Cake!" or just "WHORE-AY!" Bon appetit!

9 Sexy moves to spice up your wedding night

You've finally made it back to the hotel room and shared a much-needed bottle of champagne. Here are 9 sizzling-hot moves to jump-start your marriage from day one ...

by Steve Blake, author of *Someone's in the Kitchen with 'Gina: The Busy Couple's Guide to Green Lovemaking on a Budget.*

The Indian Scout

Spice-o-meter: ☹☹☺☺☺ Difficulty: 22

Lie on your back. Place your ears next to your ankles and listen attentively. Then say, "Five riders, about a half-mile back." Let the war whoops begin!

The Emperor Penguin

Spice-o-meter: ☺☺☺ Difficulty: 8

Have your husband lie on the bed naked, face up. Dim the lights and turn on the air conditioner. From at least 10 feet away, start running toward the bed and leap nose-forward with your arms at your sides, onto the bed, making a mo-ped sound at the top of your lungs. Vrooooom!

The Upside Down Clown

Spice-o-meter: ☹ Difficulty: 2

Put lipstick on so it appears that you have a huge frown on your face. Then bend over naked and look at him from between your legs. Guess who's smiling now?

The Dog Whisperer

Spice-o-meter: ☹☺ Difficulty: 3

Every time your husband goes to touch you, point your finger at his nose, firmly say "NO!" and make a "ch-ch-ch" sound with your mouth. As soon as he is a good boy, give him a treat: sex with you, his new wife.

The Taun-Taun

Spice-o-meter: ☹☺☹☺ Difficulty: 13

Let him ride around on your back for a while. Start making the Taun-Taun sound, "gibble gibble gibble." If you've done it right, you'll know by his having gone bananas.

The Grand Slam

Spice-o-meter: ☹☺☹☺☹☺☺☹ Difficulty: 14.88

Intersperse your lovemaking with grunts and shouts, just like Elena Marya Dmitrievnavovnaskya. Forty love!

The Virgin

Spice-o-meter: ☺☺☹☺ Difficulty: 2

Pretend that you are a virgin by asking questions like, "What's that?" and "Are we done?" and rolling around on the floor in your wedding dress, wearing lace fingerless gloves. Yum!

The Reverse Emperor Penguin

Spice-o-meter: ☹☺☹☺ Difficulty: 13

Same move as before, but add a mid-air corkscrew so you land on your back. Hint: Stick the landing and you'll be in the perfect Stargazer position; bungle it and you may end up a widow with a big ol' dent in your back!

The Croissanwich

Spice-o-meter: ☹ Difficulty: 1.618

Put on a sexy French teddy and a hide a tasty sausage biscuit somewhere in it. Mix up your verbs and let him go nuts trying to find the greasy snack of consummation.

Wedding Music, Bands, & DJ's

What's the difference between a band and a DJ?
A DJ is usually a black guy with two record players. Wedding bands are comprised of several middle-aged men.

Will the band bring their own sound system?
They don't have one, but they'll borrow one from their friend Dan, bassist for the bands Serial Baptist, Grotus Diabotus, and Blues Crawdad Incident.

What is "noodling"?
When a guitarist begins to really "feel it," he may shut his eyes and play rapid, random notes. This is called "noodling." He may also silently mouth an "owww" sound while he bends or holds longer notes—also normal.

What is a Mariachi?
You don't want this.

What is an "old lady"?
Female partner of a band member.

Is the band allowed to bring its own guests?
Not without specific permission from you. A week before the ceremony, the bassist may call you and say, "Hey, man. Hey, what about if my old lady comes?" This is acceptable. The bassist's wife will not need a vendor meal and will likely eat off of his plate or bring her own miso sandwiches.

How will the band travel to the wedding?
The band will normally arrive in a van. The guitarist will drive while the others sit on the floor in the back with equipment. The drummer may arrive later in a separate, very small car. The other members may appear mad at him, but this is normal.

We hired a five-piece band. How do we know if we're getting our money's worth?
It is your right to count band members. They may look alike, so start by dividing the band into beard/not-beard groups.

What if a band member asks if it's OK to smoke pot during the wedding?
Band members often ask this question and then laugh. You should just laugh, too, but don't answer the question.

Artwork by James Yamasaki

Dear Dean,
Thank you so much for the lovely terrarium! It's nice to get some gifts that weren't on our registry, and we had been talking about raising some big spiders or a reptile to start our marriage off. Bravo, douchebag!

♡, Mela—

Dear Teddy & Chris—
Thanks so much for the lovely 8-piece knife set. It is very nice and would be easy to divide up if, God forbid, something were to happen to our love for each other.

Cheers,
Jen and Tom

Dear Terry,
Thank you for the matching scarves. They are a beautiful reminder of our lasting marital bonds, which, as you say is "woven through eternity."
As you know,, Helen was executed at Attica on Friday. I will miss her dearly, but we enjoyed a fruitful 3-day marriage, and, to be honest, she was guilty of some pretty heinous spying crimes.
Yours,

Joe Abaya

Thank Yo

Damfeer

Darla King, Edward Carter

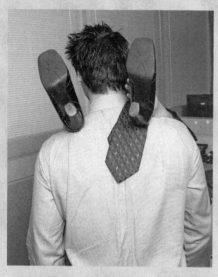

DARLA Lynn King and Edward Preston Carter were married last Saturday at a church in Los Angeles.

The couple asked a successful editor friend, who works at this newspaper, to write and publish their announcement, even though that successful editor friend wasn't asked to be a bridesmaid.

The bride, 28 (really?) is the daughter of Mr. and Mrs. King. The bridegroom, 36, is the son of Mr. Librarian and Mrs. Crane Operator.

The couple met in college, where they were considered pretty cool, but have since kind of fallen off the face of the earth.

"The wedding [sucked without Emily as a bridesmaid]," sobbed the bride. "I was just [an idiot to not ask her]. I am [so sorry]."

P.S. This is the only picture I had of you two. That is you, right Darla?

Juliet Foeller, Ronald Badgley

Juliet Foeller married Ronald Badgley on Saturday at the Founders Chapel on the campus of the University of San Diego.

Ms. Foeller, 28, is the senior director of marketing at HPY Consultants, a global investment strategy firm. She graduated *magna cum laude* from Columbia University.

Mr. Badgley, 29, is between jobs. After graduating from the University of San Diego, he worked as the assistant to Brett Chase, the film and TV producer, but quit after three months. "I got sick of all the Hollywood b---sh*t," the bridegroom said.

He was soon thereafter accepted to law school at Rutgers University, but during orientation he had second thoughts. "It just seemed like a bunch of cut-throat b---sh*t," he said. "I didn't want to be part of that scene."

He moved to New York City and tried his hand at painting

"I got sick of all the Hollywood b---sh*t," the bridegroom said.

for a while, but quickly grew jaded. "The whole art world is just a pyramid scheme," he said. "And it's so incestuous. It's full of phonies, and it's a total fucking load of b---sh*t."

Moving back to San Diego, Mr. Badgely decided he wanted to work with his hands ("real work, no b---sh*t") and found an apprenticeship at a local cabinet-maker. After a week on the job, he cut his right thumb with a lathe; a month later, he dislocated his shoulder while using a table saw.

"Yeah, woodworking was the real deal," said the groom. "No b---sh*t. But it's back to law school for this guy."

Allison Miles,
Gerald Van Bruck

Allison Miles and Gerald Van Bruck were married on Saturday at the Lido Beach Resort in Sarasota, Fla.

The couple met at the University of Pennsylvania, where they both studied economics, she graduating *summa cum laude*, he *magna cum laude*.

"*Summa cum laude* translates from the Latin as 'with highest honor' or 'with highest praise,'" said the bride. "*Magna cum laude* is a notch below, but still a great achievement. Gerald should be proud."

"If you take easier classes, like Allison did, you're going to get better grades," said the bridegroom. "And that's gonna inflate your '*cum laude*.'"

Clarissa Barnes, Jordan Gaines

Clarissa Barnes and Jordan Gaines were married at the Iglesia de San Miguel in Mexico on Thursday afternoon. A Mexican officiant performed the ceremony.

Mr. Gaines, 14-and-a-half, first met Ms. Barnes, 25, at Plainfield High School in Decatur, Ill. where she is a math teacher and basketball coach.

"She's my Baby Gurl," said the bridegroom. "So what if she's my teacher. I'm all like, 'Her chassy's off the hook and she's got the tiggo bitties.'"

Ms. Barnes agreed: "He's way ahead of all of the other seventh graders. I'm his Baby Gurl and he's my man. I even got him his own cell phone."

"She's my Baby Gurl," repeated the groom. "They say I'm the victim. I guess I am the victim—the victim of getting to bump on my teacher all the time. Hellz yeeeeaaaah!"

Natalie Pendleton, Diana Simone

VOWS

When Natalie Eloise Pendleton marries Diana Flynn Simone this Saturday on the steps of the Madison Library in Bristol, Conn, it will be a happy new chapter in a story that had the most unlikely of beginnings.

The couple, both 62, met more than four decades ago at the University of North Carolina while attending a fraternity party on campus.

"We were both dating guys in the house," recalled the bride. "They got drunk and wanted us to kiss each other."

But the women protested. "This was the South in the 1960s," explained Mrs. Simone, "and open displays of gay kissing were taboo."

So the women decided to turn the tables on the men. "Why

don't you guys kiss? We will if you will!" they said. And the guys did: Long, slow, wet, open-mouthed kisses lasting more than 40 minutes.

What followed was the widely documented "Sig Ep Flip," the 1967 incident in which an entire fraternity house became openly gay, literally overnight.

"This was the South in the '60s ... and open displays of gay kissing were taboo."

Backlash from the community followed. Parents and professors rallied to re-flip the house to hetero, and the brothers obeyed, toggling their orientation back to "straight" within one week.

Ms. Pendleton and Ms. Simone were later indicted on five counts of Instigating Gay Chaos.

"At the trial," said Ms. Pendleton, "the judge ordered us to kiss so he could 'see what all the fuss was about.' We told him that we had never kissed in the first place—we made the guys do it, and that if he wanted to know what that was like, he should kiss the prosecutor, Mr. Jake Stone."

The judge obeyed, kissing the D.A. with full tongue and even planting baby kisses on Mr. Stone's scalp and neck. While watching from the defense table, Ms. Pendleton and Ms. Simone fell in love.

Many couples are incorporating rich cultural traditions from around the world—and throughout history—into their own weddings. **Here are some of the best:**

WEDDING
Traditions

Barefoot Chazuk *(Contemporary Jewish)*. In this variation on the traditional "breaking of the glass," the shoe is removed before stomping. The Jewish groom, who is a doctor, impresses the bride's family by suturing his own foot.

No Woman, No Cry *(Rastafarian)*. When the priest asks the bride if she takes this man to be her lawful wedded husband, the bride "takes a hit of ganja." She holds the smoke in her lungs, to symbolize "thinking about it," and then exhales, and says, "I do."

Jungespiegel *(Amish)*. After the wedding, the groom becomes a pimp in Detroit for two years while the bride becomes a dancer in Vegas.

Twirl, Twirl the Rosy-O *(Medieval English)*. As the wedding guests cheer, the groom holds on to a broom and spins until his lungs fly out.

Ccochapampa *(Ancient Peruvian)*. The bride walks down a hill and sees a llama. She then walks back up, and the groom walks down and sees the llama. The bride then joins him and the three walk back up the hill. The groom then declares, "We have seen the llama and walked back with it."

Gay Cake Sharing (Gay). This is exactly the same as a hetero couple feeding each other a piece of the wedding cake except that both of the cake-eaters are gay.

The Golden Bouquet (19th century Mormon). At the end of the ceremony, as the groom watches, the bride throws her bouquet to the bridesmaids. Anyone who touches the bouquet, by law, is also married to the groom. This continues throughout the day until there are no women left.

Teotix'i'cuatl (Aztec). The entire wedding party is thrown off of a 500-foot cliff into a sparkling pool. Huge boulders are then dropped on them by priests.

Bierenhoof (Bavarian). German newlyweds will often sip from a large stein of beer through a straw made from a deer's leg. The three-legged deer is then raised by the couple until the age of four and let go: it is now time for the couple to have their own child.

Apazziatore Tamborello (Sicilian). In this Italian tradition, the groom grabs a stranger's crotch at the bus station on the morning immediately following the ceremony. When confronted, he says, "apazziatore, grazie," and is slapped.

Wolfen (Romanian). At the end of the reception, in this lively tradition, the groom will ask the bride to fetch some butter. She then leaves and is never heard from again.

T.S. Eliot Wedding (1980s English). The officiant, Old Deuteronomy, descends from the ceiling in a car tire. Everyone dresses like hobo cats.

Lighting of the Nightclub (Modern Russian). To prove his status as a provider, the Russian groom pays cash for an entire European discotheque and then torches it to the ground. An ankle-deep layer of cocaine is sometimes spread on the disco floor before burning.

Waj ab zibik (Yemeni). In Yemen, the bride's family prepares the wedding food. On the Tuesday before the wedding, the groom's family is invited to taste the feast and offer traditional criticisms, such as "The sweet fritters give the flavor of penaj" or "These date-balls taste like they were made by a Jew."

SnowMonkee, The Sun Reaper

SnowMonkee and The Sun Reaper were married Wednesday in a sunrise ceremony at the Burning Man festival in Black Rock City, Nev. The couple married themselves, which is allowed under Nevada law, in a shade structure near the ice tent.

Mr. Reaper had met Ms. Monkee the night before at Tsunami Camp, an art installation that celebrates the memory of victims of natural disasters by giving visitors ecstasy and a candle and pushing them into a plywood maze.

"I was kind of suffocating in the maze," said SnowMonkee. "I was literally candy-flopping into a soul hole."

The Sun Reaper was wearing a tool belt, and he used one of his hammers to rip an escape chute for the sunburnt single mom.

During the ceremony, The Sun Reaper manifested a tone poem on the accordion while SnowMonkee performed moon salutations. Thirty strangers attended the event, some of them wearing only gingko sheaths.

Henry VIII and Anne Boleyn

STATE OF THE UNION

10 Years Later

In January of 1533, Henry VIII and Anne Boleyn were married under complicated circumstances at a secret location in London.

So what have ten years of marriage brought to this brash and unconventional couple?

"Long story short, I cut her head off," said the king. "I mean, not me personally—I had my swordsman do it."

Gina Almassey, Rick Gottshalk

Gina Almassey married Rick Gottshalk on Saturday at the Knoxville Life Church in Knoxville, Tenn.

The couple, who have been legally blind since birth, timed their wedding to follow a revolutionary new surgery that would give them sight.

When the bride, 36, entered the chapel and laid eyes on her husband for the first time, she became sick.

"It was from the surgery," she said. "He is fine-looking. I'm just nauseous from the eye surgery."

"The surgery didn't make *me* puke," said Mr. Gottshalk, 37. "I feel 100% fine. It's almost like I got a different surgery than she did."

Melanie Bauer, Marcus Morales

Melanie Bauer and Marcus Morales will be married at the Dark Room Theater in San Francisco on Friday at midnight. Performance artist Big Jim will lead the ceremony on stage.

"Marcus is the best slam poet in the Mission district" said Ms. Bauer, 31. "When I first saw him, he was performing at this super-competitive coffee shop, Grounds for Dismissal. He was inspired; he even rhymed the word 'hegemony' with the word 'bonobo.' I almost threw my poems out that night."

"She's just being modest," said Mr. Morales, 33. "I saw her do a 90-minute improvised piece on why it's unfair that men don't have periods, or a there-would-be-no-war-if-men-had-periods type thing. Brilliant."

The two then collaborated to put on a Poetry Slam at Indian Burial Groundz, a rival coffee shop.

"We wanted to do an 'End Racism Now' show," said the bridegroom, "but it had already been done the week before by these a-holes at Coffee GroundZero. So we ended up doing 'Global Warming.'"

"He was great that night," said the bride. "I was so transfixed watching him that I didn't realize I was dumping my chai onto the Ms. Pac-Man."

Frank Alswang,
Scott Perino

Frank Alswang and Scott Perino were joined in Civil Union at the Union Civil War battlefield at Gettysburg, Pa. on Thursday.

Mr. Perino and Mr. Alswang are the cofounders of Confederates in the Closet, a "living history" organization that, through its weekend reenactments, slideshows, and private parties, imagines what it would have been like to be gay and fighting for states' rights in the 1860s.

Terri Poline, Chester Wills

Terri Poline and Chester Wills were married on Friday at the Trumpeter Evangelo-Dome in Houston Texas. The Rev. Arthur Swills performed the ceremony.

The bride and groom met at an ice cream stand at a Texas Rangers game. She ordered vanilla; he ordered chocolate.

"He's a dog person, I'm a cat person, but now he loves Snowball, and I really like his dog Oswald," said the bride.

The bride and groom's differences are most obvious when it comes to faith: She's an atheist; he's a born-again Christian.

"You know, it works out fine, except that he makes me do all the driving!" laughed the bride.

"If the Rapture comes while I'm at the wheel, the car could crash when I am taken up to heaven," said the bridegroom before suddenly turning serious. "When Johesuelah's trumpet sounds, Earth will become a hell; she'll be a slave of the Magog. The last thing she needs is a head injury to kick it all off."

Melody Parker, Dwayne Ronald Richards

Melody Parker and Dwayne Ronald Richards were married Friday at the Chapel of St. Christopher in Worcester, Mass. Rev. Mitchell Girard performed the ceremony.

The bride, 29, is an attorney who made headlines in 2006 for her defense of Joseph Dean Lewis, the so-called "Butt-Candle Bank Robber."

The groom, 36, is a night watchman.

The couple met at the bride's workplace when the groom came to see her about his case.

"I was accused of being the Dune Buggy Boner Bandit," said the groom.

"I knew Dwayne was innocent the moment I laid eyes on him," remembered the bride, "just like with Richard Lee Parker, the so-called Home Depot Gonad-Slapper.

"In the end we were able to prove to the jury that Dwayne simply couldn't maintain a hard-on in a dune buggy."

Mary Jean Stinson, Harold Grokin

Mary Jean Stinson and Lt. Harold Grokin, U.S.M.C., were married Tuesday at the St. Paul's Catholic Church in Sampson Hills, Va. The ceremony was performed by Father Norman O'Malley.

Ms. Stinson, an architecture student at New York University, is the daughter of General and Mrs. Jack "Black Jack" Stinson, the former Supreme Commander of Allied Operations in South East Asia and recipient of the Congressional Medal of Honor.

The bridegroom holds dual Master's degrees in Literature and Philosophy from Princeton University, and currently is serving in the Marine Corps with a satellite cartography unit in Okinawa.

"He is not a real soldier," joked his beaming new father-in-law, Gen. Stinson. "He would s--t his pants if he heard a f---ing firecracker. That's why Mary loves him so much: he's a real pussycat, just a real, honest-to-God pussy."

Beverly Ellis, Harold Campos

When Beverly Ellis says "I do" to Harold Campos this Saturday at the Bay Club in San Francisco, she'll be getting a new set of baggage.

Dr. Campos, 34, and Dr. Ellis, 32, both psychiatrists, met while in residency at UCLA. Initially they were rivals and had very different views on a few key subjects.

"Arguing with her was a great way to flirt," said the groom. "It was mostly in fun."

"He says that now," responded the bride. "But he's so labile. You never know which Harold is going to walk in the door: Mr. Cyclothymic-Axis-One guy? Or Mr. I-need-therapeutic-rebirthing-because-my-brother-fell-under-the-ice guy."

"That's counter-transference," said the groom. "Beverly's cluster-B stuff is going to flare up now that she's said 'I do.'"

The couple will spend their honeymoon in a Play-Combat Therapy workshop at the Nedenhauer Institute.

Rick Alpert,
Stephen Hall

When Rick Alpert and Stephen Hall first met, they felt an instant connection.

Mr. Alpert, 37, said, "I was sick of the dating scene. I had become so cynical, but when I saw Stephen—it was at the cream-and-sugar station at the coffee shop—I thought, 'This is my soul mate.'"

Mr. Hall, also 37, had similar feelings. "I was actually in a relationship at the time," he said. "But I just felt something from Rick. It was powerful, visceral. I knew he was the one."

They hit it off immediately. "We had all the same interests," recalled Mr. Alpert. "Watches, mountain biking, sports, guns, pizzas. It was uncanny."

When they revealed to each other that they were both adopted, the connection made sense. "Adopted kids just have that unique experience in common. We understand each other," said Mr. Hall.

"It turns out we even have the same birthday!" said Mr. Alpert. "Marrying him was a no-brainer."

Stephanie Worstell

STEPHANIE Lynn Worstell was married on Saturday at First Protestant Church in Monmouth, N.J.

There was no groom.

"It's time for my wedding," said the bride, 28. "It is time for my wedding."

Ms. Worstell stood at the altar next to an empty pair of black dress shoes, each with a votive candle burning in the heel, and read her own vows. "I, Stephanie, take no one to be my wedded husband," she said, smiling tearfully. "With deepest joy I come into my own life *sans homme*."

"There was a certain existential beauty to it," said Peter Collins, one of the many guests who attended the ceremony. "But that's just Stephanie's deal, you know, ever since college. She's an attention whore."

Sheila Planer,
Tom Glorel

Sheila Planer, the daughter of Vic and Sherry Planer of Norfolk, Iowa is to be married today at the Iowa City Courthouse to Tom Glorel, the son of Rich and Gladys Glorel of Reseda Seca, Nev.

Ms. Planer, 35, who is not employed, met Mr. Glorel, 34, at Reseda Seca Technical Institute, where neither of them graduated.

Mr. Glorel vowed to become a "God of the game," dropping his "ape body" to allow his "extra-sized computer" to turn into a "cosmic being." The couple said that, between the two of them, they are receiving more than 1,000 new ideas per minute.

Queen Gertrude, King Claudius

VOWS

Sometimes, great joy can come from great sorrow. That was clearly the message on Sunday, when Queen Gertrude married King Claudius at Elsinore Castle in Denmark.

Just weeks before, the royal family—and all of Denmark—had been reeling from the untimely death of Gertrude's first husband, King Hamlet, Sr.

"What a shock. Nothing can prepare you for that," said best man, Polonious. "True, the funeral baked meats *did* coldly furnish forth the wedding table, but why waste good reindeer?"

The theme of the day was The Circle of Life, with toast after toast referring to the miracle of turning "tragedy" into

---

... turning tragedy into "tragetunity" ...

"tragetunity." In fact, more than one reveler pointed out how divine it was that the queen had room in her heart to fall in love with her brother-in-law.

The queen's son, Hamlet, Jr., seemed to be in top spirits, traipsing around the banquet hall, finishing half-drunk goblets of wine. "He's really taking this well," said Claudius. "I thought he would be upset that I was with his mother. But he's been a cool stepson so far."

The only tense moment of the weekend occurred when Queen Gertrude's bouquet was caught by young Ophelia. After grabbing the flowers, she flipped out and drowned in the pond.

Also, just a short while later, everyone else was dead.

How many brides can say that?

Jessica Richmond
George Molindo

Jessica Richmond and George Molindo were married at the Scripps County Fairgrounds in French Glen, Ore. on Friday. The Rev. Thomas Wilmot officiated.

The couple has a very special claim to fame: both are listed in the Guinness Book of World Records and met at a gathering for world-record holders in Dublin, Ireland several years ago.

"It was amazing," said the bridegroom, 42. "I saw all of these people that I remembered from reading the book as a kid. There was the fingernail guy; the huge twins on the motorcycles; the man with the super long moustache ... and then there was Jessica."

"It is a special bond, I have to say, and it's a great conversation starter," laughed the bride, 36. "Of course my first question was 'What's your world record?' And he told me that he rode a unicycle across Europe and I was like, 'Wow.'"

"And I asked, 'What's yours?'" said Mr. Molindo. "And she said she'd been pregnant 112 times. It's a very different kind of record than plate-spinning or eating a bicycle. It's just different. That's a lot of dudes. A lot of dudes."

You don't know me, but PLEASE pay close attention: the picture above is just there to get your attention. Sorry. Ignore it. I am trapped in the basement of *The New York Times* building in Manhattan. RIGHT NOW. THIS MOMENT. I'm kept here and forced to write wedding announcements. My captors are bitches: they keep me here and feed me Grape-Nuts. They whip me in the ass with a loofah. They tell me wrong things: A LOT OF THESE NEWLYWEDS DID NOT GRADUATE *CUM LAUDE*. Oh great, now there's a bee in here, too! Nothing works out for me. You know what, don't call 911. I'll just deal with it myself like always. I'm sorry I bummed everyone out.

Tiffany Jennings
Gary Mollford

Tiffany Jennings and Gary Mollford were married Saturday at Lakeside Chapel in Milwaukee.

The bridegroom, 38, who is a Milwaukee Brewers fan, surprised the bride by proposing to her via a message on the stadium's JumboTron: "Tiffany, Will You Marry Me?"

"People started cheering," said Ms. Jennings, 33. "At first I thought, 'That's probably some other Tiffany.'"

Mr. Mollford then dug his thumb into her Polish sausage to reveal an engagement ring that he had hidden within.

"Every girl wants to be proposed to on the Jumbo-Tron," said Ms. Jennings. "Especially when she gets a kielbasa with a cubic zirconium stuffed into it. Holy shit."

CORRECTIONS

Melanie Burger, Douglass Atwal. The wedding announcement for Melanie Burger and Douglass Atwal misstated the location of their first date. He took her to The Crepe Vine, not The Date Crepe.

Maria Dancy, Carlos Henninger. The "State of the Union" feature on Maria Dancy and Carlos Henninger reported that they have been happily married for 10 years. The article should have stated that they were happy during the first, second, fifth, seventh, and ninth years.

Sonya Babcock, Miles Padovano. The wedding announcement for Sonya Babcock and Miles Padovano incorrectly referred to the bridegroom as "Doctor Padovano" and to his book as *Zen and the Healing Touch.* His correct title is *Former Doctor* Padovano and his book is titled *Cocaine is My Master.*

Gloria Haynes, Andrew Pleasance. Inexplicably, a report on the marriage of Gloria Haynes and Andrew Pleasance neglected to mention that the bride's father was 8th in his class at Andover in 1956. Jesus. Sorry.

CORRECTIONS

Vanessa Chalmers, Robert Patterson. An announcement of the marriage of Vanessa Chalmers and Robert Patterson misspelled the following words: "Chalmers," "Patterson," "Montauk," "bipolar," "punched," "raccoon," "Taser," and "jail."

Christy Peters, Gary John Daniels. A report on the marriage of Christy Peters and Gary John Daniels incorrectly stated that the wedding was a "festive rural affair incorporating the unique rhythms of farm life." It should have stated that the wedding was "ruined by a donkey falling off of a cliff."

Valerie Beeman, Charles DeRossi. A report on the marriage of Valerie Beeman and Charles DeRossi incorrectly stated that the father of the bridegroom was "stripped of a bronze medal in the backstroke." It should have read that he "broke his back stripping bronze metal and had a stroke."

Wendy Dahl, Zack Laberenz. The photo accompanying the wedding announcement for Wendy Dahl and Zack Laberenz was not of the bride and groom; it was an eighteenth-century political cartoon captioned, "A woolvyrine eating the mayor's arse-hole."

Artwork by James Yamasaki

About the Authors

Kasper Hauser (L to R), John Reichmuth, Dan Klein, James Reichmuth, and Rob Baedeker, are San Francisco-based comedy writers and performers and the authors of *SkyMaul: Happy Crap You Can Buy from a Plane*.

www.kasperhauser.com

Acknowledgments

We would like to thank the following people for their help with this book:

Our agent, Danielle Svetcov, who endured many late-night phone calls, laughed with us, cried with us, and shared in our many, many triumphs; our editor, Peter "Pete" Joseph, who also did that; the friends and fans of Kasper Hauser who bravely submitted or posed for photos, even photos we couldn't include because the people were not smartly dressed; our families, Michelle, Ben, Laura, Nora, Andrea, and Julie, who manned the phones and went door-to-door canvassing for support when people said we couldn't do it—that a comedy troupe couldn't put a black man in the White House; to Vince, Jen, Jack, and Clara for designing this book as a family, even when the children were forced to homeschool as a result; to James "Jimmy" Yamasaki for painting the beautiful pictures that gave life to our vision; to Brad Rhodes for using a computer to enhance the pornography; to Walk C. Jones IV, Paul Stasi, Gabe Weisert, Denis Faye, Ross McCall, Mo Lee, and Marisa Milanese, who sometimes gently, sometimes bluntly, but always honestly, told us how funny this book was; to fellow artists and comics John Hodgman, Patton Oswalt, Bob Odenkirk, Laura Silverman, Todd Barry, Ben Karlin, Will Reiser, Jesse Thorn, Michelle Biloon, Alexandra Matthew, Chris Hardwick, Dave Owen, Janet Varney, Cole Stratton, and SF Sketchfest, for risking their lives, living in barns in the French countryside, and learning perfect German to ensure that Hitler's mad dream did not become a nightmare for the whole world; and finally, Charles "Chaz" Abramovitz, the so-called "boy band" producer who found each of the members of Kasper Hauser, one in a mall, one at a Pop Warner football game, and two at a 4-H donkey auction, got us the haircuts, the clothes, and the tour bus, and wrote all of the catchy comedy hooks that would mold us into who we are, Kasper Hauser, the Comedy Group.

Photo/Copyright Credits